You'll Need to be Brave

L.W. Eells

Table of Contents

Acknowledgments

I want to thank the Lord for this story. How He guided me through the darkness to the light. I want to thank Him for His grace and love.

I also want to thank my wife for the endless hours of help on this project. Without her, I wouldn't have been able to finish this book.

And for Alice. Thank you so much for your time, help, and guidance. You gave me the courage to just go for it and start writing.

Lastly, thank you so much, reader, for giving this book a chance. I hope you find the journey interesting and inspiring.

1

The Beginning

How do I write the story of my life? Where do I begin?

I have been told my story is very unique and interesting. I don't know about that, but what I do know is my life's been quite a journey. A journey through many storms, many dark days. A journey towards a light and a life I could never imagine. My story isn't really my story, it's actually God's story... it's a story that He's allowed me to be a part of.

Well... I guess I should start at the beginning.

My mom was from California originally, but moved to Eugene, Oregon when she was in high school to live with her grandparents. My mom came from a broken home. Her mother was a mess. She'd had many kids from many different fathers. My mom's dad was a good man but couldn't stay with a woman who wouldn't be faithful. To me, it sounded like my mom's time with her grandparents in Eugene was the most stable and peaceful time of her life up to that point. My mom was a beautiful blonde with a big smile. It is easy to see why my dad was drawn to her. He was working at the local McDonald's, and she was sent there to help McDonald's debut the new Filet-O-Fish Sandwich in 1966. My dad asked her out and they fell in love.

The Vietnam War was starting to heat up and my dad decided to join the U.S. Coast Guard instead of being drafted into the army.

Before he went to bootcamp, my mom got pregnant with my older sister. Due to the circumstances, they eloped with another couple to Utah to get married.

After they returned to Eugene and the dust settled, my dad went to bootcamp, and my mom went to live with my dad's parents. My sister was born at the hospital while my dad was at the North Pole. It even made the local newspapers when he was able to return on leave to meet her for the first time. I think those were good years. My mom and her new baby girl. Her own little family. Something she had always wanted.

My dad returned on leave a year later and got sick while he was at home. They went to the hospital and learned my dad needed surgery and a few weeks' rest before he could return to active duty. While he was healing up in the hospital his aunt visited him with a cousin and an elder from the Followers of Christ Church in Oregon City. The leader of the church had prophesied that the end of time was near, and everyone in the church needed to go out and gather everyone they knew who needed to be saved. Being saved, to the Followers, meant joining that church and being baptized by their leader. After much discussion, my dad decided he needed to go back to the church and get baptized.

My dad had been in the church when he was a young boy, but my mom had never been a member, nor did she have any family attending either. Still, she joined the church alongside her husband. Now my mom had a little family and a new church. Things were looking up. Her husband soon got out of the Coast Guard and that's when my story starts.

I was born on July 2, 1970. My parents had recently joined a church that was actually a cult. The church didn't allow you to go to the doctor, so my mother had me at home with a midwife.

After I was born, times were tough for my mom. She struggled with fitting in at the church, not having any family there. I think she had postpartum depression too. I've heard so many conflicting stories about my mom during that time, I don't really know what to believe anymore. What I do know is, she loved us, my sister and me. I think she really tried to be a good mother.

Little did we know things were about to take a horrible turn. A dark turn that would drastically affect the rest of our lives.

2

The Church

What is a cult? How do you define it? Google defines a cult as "a relatively small group of people having religious beliefs or practices regarded by others as strange or sinister."

How do you know if you're in a cult? Just try and leave it without being punished or shunned. If you're shunned or punished for leaving, or even for asking questions about leaving, then you'll know you're definitely in a cult.

The Followers of Christ Church, I believe, fits the description of what a cult is. The Followers of Christ Church was started in the mid to late 1800s in the eastern part of America, roughly around the same time the Mormon church started. The Followers and Mormon churches had very similar ideas and traditions, and figuratively walked next to each other through the 1800s. The Followers were even accused of being an offshoot of the Mormon Church by the newspapers of the time. Where the Mormon Church took off, the Followers church did not. It slowly crept across the country during the same time that many other churches started in America.

The Followers had/have many traditions that would have seemed very odd to most people back then, and especially in modern times. Back in the church's beginnings, the Followers held to the "signs and wonders" that were written in Mark 16:9-20, such as snake handling, speaking in tongues, drinking poison without sickness, and faith healing. There are newspaper articles going back to the late 1800s that talk about children dying due to the Followers not seeking medical help.

Sadly, even to this day, children have continued to die because their parents refuse to seek medical attention for them. It's been the tradition, from the early days until modern times, that if you do seek medical attention, you could be shunned out of the church by the leadership or the members. But more importantly, if you seek medical attention, it's believed that you will lose your salvation.

Although snake handling isn't practiced anymore, it was taught, even up to my generation, that if you had enough faith (not faith in Jesus, just faith, which is used very broadly), you could pick up a snake and it would go straight as a stick and not harm you. Many traditions at the church have made the Followers more and more closed off from the outside world.

For various reasons, all the existing Followers churches have separated themselves from one another. I think it's because each of the churches think they are living closer to what they hold as truth or tradition. Each church thinks they are better than the other. This slowly happened throughout the middle of the 1900s. The separation and closing of themselves off to the world has caused so much hurt and confusion.

The Oregon City church was, and still is, the largest of all the Followers churches. At its peak, there were roughly around 2000 members.

All the Follower churches are slowly fading away as they wait for the end of time to come. Most have lost their leaders and are dwelling in traditional darkness, not knowing Jesus, thinking they can work their way into heaven…maybe… if they have enough faith.

Traditionally, the preacher has to be "called" to the position. This can be by another preacher or "called man," but some were "called" by what they perceived as a revelation from God and then affirmed by the current preacher or "called man." Walter White was the last "called man" or leader of the Oregon City church. He figuratively closed the doors to the outside world in 1968 and didn't appoint another "called man" because he had prophesied the end of time was near. I guess he was right in a way; he died in 1969. The end of his time did happen, but for the congregation this almost made things worse. They looked at his prophecy as partly being fulfilled and the rest as it was coming soon. Since Walter died in 1969, you have to be born into the church and no one can join from the outside world, because there is no way to baptize you into the church. Baptisms had to be done by a "called man", and the last "called man" had died.

Many families have been in the church for generations which causes issues of its own. They have stopped looking to the Bible for truth, if they ever did. They rely on the traditions passed on from their grandpas or dads. These traditions are based heavily on what the leader said the Bible said, not even what the Bible actually does say. Typically, these are verses taken out of context and made into a tradition.

The Followers believe they are the only ones who get a chance to go to heaven, because they're the only true chosen people of God. Everyone outside of the church is considered to be "the world." The Followers are a semi-hidden community within the city that they live in. Basically, they keep to themselves except for going to public school or doing business with "the world". When you're a part of the church you don't really interact with "the world." You go to school with "the world" and you work in "the world," but you have to keep a distance from everyone you interact with. We were taught we had to hide our faith and who we were, because "the world" just wouldn't understand.

Why? Because what if you get to be friends with someone outside of the church? Then what? They wouldn't be allowed to join the church; you have to be born into it. There is also a chance that friendship might pull you out of the church. You also can't play sports at school either, that may also draw you out and what if you get hurt? The coach or school authorities would take you to the hospital and that would be dangerous to your faith, and possibly to your salvation.

The shunning of medicine is a big part of being a Follower. The Followers of Christ Church is a faith healing church. We were warned against going to the doctor or to the hospital. To the Followers, faith is defined as having enough belief in God that you will be healed. There is no understanding of faith as defined in the gospel, believing that Jesus Christ died on the cross for your sins. They believe if you have enough of this healing faith, that God will heal you. If you don't...well, He might not. But ultimately it is His will. If you get sick and die a slow and painful death without seeking medical intervention, many people say that you've earned your crown in heaven due to the suffering you've endured. They use the Bible verse Mark 8:35: *"For whoever would seek to save his life will lose it, but whoever loses his life for my sake and the gospel's will save it."* They interpret this as if you seek to save your physical life with a doctor, you'll lose your spiritual life.

The Followers cherry-pick verses out of the Bible to try and shore up their traditions without really looking at the context of what the Bible verse is actually teaching. Followers also believe that you have to earn your way into heaven by doing good works, but only good works to those who go to the Followers church. They believe the only way to please God and earn your way into heaven is by doing all of the traditions that are taught. But the most important rule is, DO NOT leave the church. If you leave the church, it's taught that you will definitely go to hell.

We were called Followers of Christ, but we knew very little about Jesus or the Holy Spirit, forget the idea of what the Trinity is. The Bible is talked about, but I don't think many people actually read it very much. Jesus isn't really taught either. We knew He was the Son of God, and died on the cross, but for what reason? We didn't know. We didn't understand, or even know about, the saving grace of the cross. We would end a prayer in Jesus' name but didn't really know why. I was told it's because Jesus was God's Son and if we used His name, God might listen. If you didn't end the prayer in Jesus' name, God wouldn't hear the prayer at all. It would basically fail to send.

It was at the direction of the leader, Walter, in the late 1960s, that people went out and gathered loved ones to come back to the church, before the doors were figuratively closed to the outside world. This is how my parents were drawn into the church.

Shortly after joining, my dad brought a Bible to church, and he was met with hostility. Walter said, "Who does he think he is, bringing a Bible into this church?! What is he going to do, check up on ME?!" This is how my dad was rebuked from the pulpit.

I heard about this my entire life, not from my dad, but from other members of the church. "How dare he!" I was told.

Doesn't that seem odd? Being rebuked for bringing a Bible into a church?

If you're a Follower who does read the Bible, who studies and wants to talk about Scripture (and most don't), it is looked at as if you're trying to exalt yourself. This is met with negativity that somehow you will be perceived as being at a higher place or status in the community. That would make you stand out or not fit in. And you must fit in. Conforming to the perceived social norms, and keeping everyone around you in their place, is where the members of the church use the power of shunning and fear against one another like a weapon.

After the death of the leader, Walter White, the elders in the church took over and everyone waited for the end of time to come. In 1986 the last elder died, and a group of men took over. They're called the Board. They run things now. At a church meeting, there are no sermons preached, there is no Bible read, only ten hymns were sung twice a week, and that's it and that's all.

Remember I asked what is a cult, and how do you define it? As I said, Google defines a cult as "a relatively small group of people having religious beliefs or practices regarded by others as strange or sinister." This description fits, doesn't it?

I hope this helps to build a picture of the world I was born into.

A community within a community. A closed off world, a world of traditions that don't make sense most of the time. A world where you have to strive to be at the top of the heap. A place where you can't be anything but perfect and if you are a little bit different, you're treated as if you are less and pushed down and stood on, so everyone else can stand a little higher.

Tradition and peer pressure rule that place, not truth. Not Jesus.

3

◆

Our Lives Will Never Be the Same

One chilly winter day, my mom was walking home from the bus stop with a load of groceries. She had to walk about half a mile from the bus stop to our home. We lived down a country road, a road without sidewalks and not much of a shoulder. It was a typical country road with a slight hill rising up towards our house. There was just a ditch alongside the road for refuge if a log truck or fast-moving car came by. She'd made the trek many times, walking to catch the bus to town and back again, carrying whatever was needed for the home.

She had to use the bus, due to my dad not allowing her to get a driver's license. She was so thankful the bus stop was only a half mile walk and not farther. She enjoyed getting out of the house and seeing the sites and goings on. Most of the time, she had two little children in tow, herding those kids like a mother hen, as she carried as many bags as she could manage.

Many people have told me about seeing her with her little kids walking on that country road and thinking how dangerous it was, a two-year-old and a five-year-old plus bags of groceries. They said it wouldn't have surprised them if they'd heard that we'd been hit by a car.

On this winter day, my mom was alone. Her mother-in-law had

offered to watch the kids when she went to town. My mom was thankful for the break because her mind was full of distractions, and her heart was broken.

As she walked, she was thinking about how she was going to save her marriage. She had recently found out my dad was having an affair with a girl from the bank. When she confronted my dad, it didn't go well, as you can imagine. My dad wanted to hide it from everyone at the church so as to not lose his standing there, and what was worse, he didn't act like it was a big deal. He treated my mom like she was his property, not his wife. She had suspected something was going on with my dad, not only with the girl from the bank, but with an old high school girlfriend who was now living in the area as well.

When I spoke to my dad years later about why he'd done that, not only to my mom, but to my sister and me as well, he said, "The girl at the bank was so nice."

"SHE WAS SO NICE?!" I shouted. He still acted like my mom's feelings weren't an issue because she didn't really matter.

My mom was already feeling a distance with the church. She'd tried to make friends, but it was hard. She wasn't raised in the church, and the traditions and customs seemed a little odd to her. She wanted to fit in, but how could she hide what her husband was doing? Who could she talk to about it? Who would understand? She felt lost and alone. She'd hoped that if they kept it between just themselves, they could get through it and move on. But the arguments had been getting more and more heated.

In one of the fights, a glass ash tray was thrown against the wall and broke, falling behind the couch where my sister and I were hiding from the yelling. My foot was badly cut as I tried to run from the crashing glass. This only made things worse, as each blamed one another for the injury. It was like we were in a storm.

My mom had already lived through a storm just like this, a storm of her childhood, with her mother and father raging at each other... only in that storm, her mother was the one who wouldn't be faithful. Now, it was her husband. How could he do this to her, her heart cried out? Her life was coming unraveled. Her little family dream was imploding.

The long walk home in the cold was almost over. That's when her heart stopped as she turned and entered the driveway. Why were there so many cars at her house? And what was the sheriff's car there for? My mom froze in place for a second; all she could think was, "Oh please Lord, not my babies!"

She started running towards the house, her heart breaking with every step. She couldn't breathe and could only get out a "No—no—no, Lord, please!" as she rushed past the cars to the house. She was met at the door by a sheriff's deputy.

He said to her, "You can't come in!" Her mind was frantic with fear. All she could do was try and push past him. He grabbed her and said, "You can't enter this house!"

"My babies!" she cried out. "Where are my babies?" The tears were flowing down her cheeks, and her mind was spinning. Why was he stopping her? What had happened? Was it so bad that he was trying to stop her from seeing her dead children?

"My babies..." Her voice shook. "Are they dead?" The words

almost burned as they left her mouth. "Oh Lord please not my babies!" she sobbed.

The world started spinning and she felt weak. Her heart was beating so fast it felt like it would explode, her eyes were a blur with tears. That's when the deputy grabbed her, looked her in the eyes, and said, "It's not your babies! There is a restraining order against you, and you have to leave NOW!"

Wait... what? Her mind didn't process what the deputy was saying. Where were her babies? "Are they OK?" she asked.

The deputy said, "Ma'am your children are OK, but you have to leave."

"Leave? And go where?" Nothing was making sense.

"I don't care where you go, but you can't be here," he said.

Over the deputy's shoulder, my mom could see my dad and his older brother sitting at the kitchen table. My uncle wouldn't look at my mom. She told me that he looked so sheepish as he stared at his feet, looking like he was completely filled with guilt. My dad had a defiant look on his face, as he just stared at my mom. Her mother-in-law wasn't anywhere to be seen, and she couldn't hear her babies' voices as she called out for us.

"They're not here," the deputy told my mom. He told her that he would go with her to her room to pack one small bag with a few clothes, but after that she would be escorted off the property and arrested if she returned.

Her fear and panic turned to rage! "Where are my children and WHY DO I HAVE TO LEAVE?"

The deputy said to her that he didn't have the answers to those questions, but he had a job to do. "So please Ma'am, please just fill your bag and go."

My dad just sat there looking at her as she passed him. He had an *I won* look on his face. Her rage burned hot. What had he done? What lies had he told the police? Where were her babies? And... how could he do this to her?

The deputy helped my mom put a few clothes, and only clothes, into her bag. No pictures, no keepsakes; nothing but the clothes and the coat on her back. He walked with her to the end of the driveway. My mom said, "I have no money and nowhere to go."

The deputy said to her, "I really am sorry Ma'am, if you have nowhere to go, you could try the YMCA, they take in women for the night that are in need."

She could barely get out an "OK" as she staggered back down the country road she had just come from. Her feet felt like they were made of lead. Her breath was short, and her heart was broken beyond belief. As the cars passed her with a whoosh, the dust stuck to the tears that were running down her face.

My mom told me that at that moment she wished a truck would have run her over and ended her pain. I can picture her walking in the cold with her coat not quite on, the bag she had packed dragging the ground as she walked in shock towards the unknown. Her heart broken and her mind blank.

Somehow, she made it to the bus stop. The driver helped her to town and guided her to the YMCA that was in the next town over. Just like the deputy had told her, they took my mom in and gave her a cot and one blanket for the night. She was shown to a large room that was empty except for her and her cot.

She was glad in a way that the room was empty because she couldn't stop weeping. Her heart was shattered, and her head was pounding, but what was most troubling to her was the pain she felt inside. A pain down low, a pain where her unborn baby was. She had recently found out she was pregnant but hadn't told my dad yet. She was waiting for the right time, the right moment, hoping this might help their troubles to pass. But now… now what? She felt a defiance build in her. A defiance, a strength in her saying, my dad may have stolen her other children from her, but he wouldn't get this one! "Not this one!" she thought. "This one's mine!"

It gave her something to cling to, a hope for a future. Sadly, her hopes would soon be dashed. Maybe because of the trauma and stress of that day or the days to come, but sadly, she lost that baby too.

She told me later that that night on the cot at the YMCA, in that big room alone, was the worst day of her life. She had lost everything…her children, her husband, the life she had known. Her whole world had imploded. She had no money and no one.

Now what? She didn't know.

4

$\blacklozenge$

His Evil Plan

My dad's plan had worked perfectly. My mom was broken, and he had successfully run her off. He and his mother had come up with a devious plan to hide my dad's sin, and make my mom out to be a crazy, dangerous person that her kids couldn't be around. Who would argue with that? No one really knew my mom at the church, she'd only been a member for a couple of years, and she didn't have any family there to support her, either. People began to whisper that my mom's mother was a mess, so why wouldn't she be that way too?

This lie went through the rumor mill at the church like a wildfire. "She was crazy, evil and a liar," my grandma and my dad told everyone. But worst of all, they said she wanted to leave the church. That story would definitely get people on my dad's side. Remember, leaving the church was the worst thing anyone could do. If you did leave, you were shunned and looked at as dangerous and people at the church weren't supposed to speak with you.

This was a perfectly evil plan. She was gone and no one could ask her for her side of the story. Only my dad's narrative was to be heard, and he played the victim very well. My grandmother was telling that story far and wide to anyone who would listen. My grandmother was an evil woman. She was a master of manipulation, a complete narcissist. No woman was going to come between her and her son. She jumped at the opportunity to get her place back.

Get rid of the wife and my dad would need her again. She didn't care what he was up to, it actually played into her hand perfectly. If she had something over him, she had power over him, too.

After putting all the pieces together later in my life, I confronted my dad about this. He admitted it all to me. Yes, he had run my mom off to hide what he was doing. He was tired of hearing how upset she was that he was messing around. My grandmother and my dad had hatched this plan when they thought my mom was going to go public with the information. He couldn't have his name muddied at the church. I remember what he had said to me about the girls he'd been messing around with: "They were so nice." He didn't see his actions as a sin. He was just a male version of his mother; a complete narcissist just like her. A slick womanizer with a "use them and lose them" attitude.

But now he had a problem: two little kids. What was he going to do with them? He didn't really want us, but he needed us as leverage over my mom to keep her quiet. He couldn't get rid of us. Plus, he liked the attention he was getting at the church as the poor, single father. "Oh, look at how great of a father he is," they'd say as he walked into church with his kids all cleaned up and their hair combed. Little did they know my sister and I were living with my grandparents.

The ladies were extra nice to him now. He could go to work and then go out with his flings, and no one was giving him grief about it. He was living the life he wanted. But soon, they were going to court for custody of the kids in the divorce. This was going to be public. "Oh no! What might she say on the stand?" he worried. Did his plan have a flaw?

The church was going to help with the financial part of the attorney fees due to my dad being the "victim." What if they found out about his messing around? That would ruin his narrative and well-laid plans. My dad and grandma would need to increase the "She's a liar" propaganda, but would that be enough? No, they needed more!

People were hearing my sister and I were staying with our grandparents, and my dad was living alone at his house. People were starting to question where my dad was. He needed something to shore up that he was a good guy, just getting by. He needed a new wife... or at least a girlfriend that everyone at the church would see so it would appear that he was moving on with his life. A girlfriend people wouldn't question.

But who? Who would want to take on two little kids? A ready-made family that was in limbo, a family still going to court. Was the judge going to give the kids to the mother? How involved was the mother going to be in the kids' lives? So many unanswered questions that hadn't been decided yet. Who would want the job?

Oh wait... what about the babysitter? She was an older single girl from the church. Her family wasn't thought too highly of either. Maybe she might be desperate for a husband.

At the Followers church, if you're a girl older than twenty, you are considered an "older girl" and not looked at by the young boys as marrying material. If you hadn't snagged a husband by seventeen, there must be something wrong with you. The older girls are viewed as damaged goods.

Yes, the babysitter might be perfect! The kids liked her...at least they seemed to. My dad told me, "She was good with the kids and a blond." That was good enough for him. He didn't love her, he told me; he just needed a replacement for my mom, the woman he'd run off.

My dad had a highly paid lawyer, and my mom had a lawyer appointed by the court. My mom lost. No surprise there. She was given limited visitation, and it had to be supervised. They'd convinced the judge she was a threat. She had no one in her defense and the church had many people willing to lie on the stand to "protect the kids from the world."

And just like that…my mom was gone. The day the divorce was finalized, my dad married the babysitter. If this was a movie, this is where the really ominous music would start. Ominous and dark.

That dark storm that we'd been living in for so long just got much, much worse.

5

$\blacklozenge$

The Darkness

At the church we attend now, once a month, there's a big plastic jug up by the pulpit that the little kids run up to to put in the coins they've been collecting. You can't help but smile at all the little ones joyfully giving to help the children's ministry. The church sanctuary is large, fanning out from the front where the pulpit sits.

One Sunday, not long ago, I was seated about five or six rows back, in the middle aisle. After the little ones get done putting in their coins, they run back to their seats, with big smiles on their faces, so happy they've completed their task.

This day, a little boy started running up the aisle I was on and then suddenly stopped not far from where I was seated. I watched him as he realized he was lost. You could see the panic come over him as he spun around, eyes wide, searching for anything that looked familiar. His poor little face was frantic as he cried out "MAMA!"

He was lost and where was his mama, his brain was crying out in panic. "MAMA!" he cried. Over his shoulder, I could see a woman rushing through the pews almost stepping on the people that were in her way, his mother.

"MAMA!" the little boy cried out again, frozen in place. Panic had rooted him to the ground where he stood.

His mother called back to him, "I'm here," as she almost stumbled in her haste to reach him. "I'm here."

The child spun around looking in the direction of his mother's call. "MAMA!" he called back as she reached him. His mother scooped him up and held him close, his legs and arms wrapped around her, burying his face into her neck.

"I'm here," I heard her softly say as they walked out of the sanctuary.

The next part of my story is going to be really hard to write about. I'm sorry to you the reader because it's going to be really hard to read as well. Just know… it was even harder to live through.

I've been avoiding thinking about writing this part of my story. As I walk through the memories and stories of the start of my life, I've tried to not notice the other memories that lingered at the edge of my mind. Memories that haunt me like a hooded figure standing at the end of my driveway. A hooded figure just standing there, staring at me… A faceless dark mass of memories that moves into the shadows when I turn to confront it.

How am I going to write about things I can barely face? Will it help me, or will it break me?

Lord please be with me as I face the dark, evil, brutal memories of my past.

Child abuse is a hidden scourge in this world. Sadly, children are made to fear or feel guilty about telling anyone about the abuse they've endured. But more often, the kids are made to feel like they deserve what's happening to them.

Both are horrible things for a child to endure. The fear and the guilt. It messes with the foundation of a child's mind. Their world is like living between the trenches of World War I, living in "No Man's Land" as a battle rages around them. Nowhere to run. Nowhere to hide.

Physical abuse leaves scars you can see. Mental abuse leaves the same number of scars, if not worse, but those scars...those scars are much harder to see. I have both.

I'm not sure what I should write about and what I should leave out. If I don't talk about the depths of abuse, how will you know how dark the darkness was? The darkness was very deep, but the light that's to come is so much brighter. It's brighter because of it... because of the darkness.

How can I write that this is God's story? Horrible dark abuse and God in the same lines? I know, it took me awhile to realize that God was there with me the entire time. That, for whatever reason, He allowed me to endure the abuse. I'm not mad at God. I don't look back angrily and say, "Why God?" I don't know... somehow, I have a peace with God, knowing He was there with me.

I hope that you see Him in my story in the darkest moments giving me hope or comfort, but we'll have to get through a lot of stuff together, you and me.

Yes, you the reader. Knowing you're there helps me in an odd way. It helps me to know you're there helping me as I put on my armor. I don't feel so alone as I'm readying my mind to venture back. I can almost taste the blood in my mouth, mixed with the tears. But the fear... the fear is the hard one to face. So, thank you reader. Thank you for the support. If it gets too bad, just close the book for a while, close it to give us both a rest. But please, please don't leave me there for too long alone...

Okay, ready? Okay, let's go.

My first memories are mere flickers of photos, nothing I can put context to. These memories are more feelings with images attached. Feelings of fear, and just like that little boy at church, a feeling of panic and a need to cry out "MAMA!"

But my mother never came to scoop me up. I was alone and lost in my heart. Fear and panic are the first scars that marked me. Fear and panic, and a never-ending search for my mother.

Fear and pain became close friends as I grew from a toddler to a little boy. I had a fear of my dad mixed with a need for his love and approval, but my stepmother was totally different. With her, I was always afraid. I don't want to give her the satisfaction of being called *my* stepmother, so I'll just call her "The Stepmother."

My dad was of the mindset, "a child should be seen but never heard," and he wasn't afraid to use his belt so you would remember it. The Stepmother was just evil. She thought children were put on this earth for her to torture, regardless of if they were quiet or not. She would think of very interesting ways to keep me afraid of her and her wrath. She had a darkness about her and a hatred you could see in her eyes. Let's just say she was a very "hands on" disciplinarian.

She was a stocky woman with a mean right hook. "Why slap when you can punch instead?" was her way of thinking. You could never predict when she would attack. Typically, a blow would come from the side or from behind. It could be a slap or a punch, and sometimes it would be a kick or a handful of hair being pulled out of your head. Always an overreaction, always an attack meant to wound.

Love was something that was foreign in the house that I grew up in. Love was a weakness that wouldn't be tolerated. It was met with hate, pain, and tears. My dad had run off my mother and married a monster who was bent on killing any love I had in me, but she couldn't take away the only love I had left in my life: Sissy.

My older sister and I were very close during those early years. She is three years older than I am, and I loved her. I called her Sissy. She took care of me a lot of the time, playing with me and sneaking me snacks when I was hungry. She would try and help me when I was scared and coach me on how to stay out of the line of sight when The Stepmother was on a rant. I learned to be very quiet and watchful. It changed my personality, I think. I know how a deer feels in a forest of wolves, always on the alert, always ready to run for my life. It's a hard way to live. It's not really living, it's existing.

Fear, pain, and Sissy were my world. It was me and her against the fearful darkness we lived in. Together, we just might survive.

Sissy took the brunt of many beatings on my behalf. I think she did it to protect me. If I spilled my milk on accident or any other normal thing a three-year-old boy might do, she'd sometimes take the blame for me. I was so afraid for her, and I would cry when I could hear her getting a beating.

When I say beatings, I want you to understand it wasn't a typical spanking as you might have had when you were little. No, the beatings I'm talking about were brutal beatings. Typically, The Stepmother would have us by the hair, jerking us back and forth, as she used her grasp as a handle to pull us towards her as she hit us, not only with her hands, but with whatever she had at hand. The blows often landed from your heels to the back of your head.

Beatings that really hurt, not just stung, often leaving bruises that we had to hide or lie about.

As I grow older in the story, you'll see the beatings get much, much worse—I'm talking peeing blood worse. They were way more intense and brutal, and the objects that were used to beat me with will probably shock you. A few times, I tried to reach out for help from people I knew and thought wouldn't snitch on me that I was telling, but sadly, it seems people do not want to believe a parent figure can do horrible things to a child. Beating a child bloody just shuts people down, and they would turn away like I was telling lies.

It's really odd. If a child comes to you and reaches out for help, please believe them. It's not up to you to fix it, it's up to you to report it. These days it is much easier to report child abuse. Just make a call. You might save a life.

During those early years we rented a house on a large sheep farm. My grandfather had managed the farm until he retired, that's when we moved in. Sissy and I had already lived there with our grandparents during the divorce. My grandparents moved out and we moved in.

My dad didn't work the farm, we just rented the house that was on the property. The house was a smaller house, but not tiny. It had three bedrooms on the west side of the house and a living room, with the kitchen and bathroom just through an opening on the east side.

My room was in the front corner and Sissy's room was the next room over. We would often have to play alone in our rooms because of some unknown punishment. I think The Stepmother hated that

Sissy and I were close. She was jealous and it made her even meaner towards us, but especially towards me.

Sissy and I would talk through the heating vent in the floor. We would talk about how unhappy we were and how we missed our real mother. Little did we know, The Stepmother could hear us as well. She would burst into our rooms and scream at us to stop talking to each other, but it didn't stop our conversations.

One day, little red plastic phones showed up in our rooms. They plugged into the wall and a wire ran under the door, behind the couch and to Sissy's room. If I wanted to talk to her when we were confined to our rooms, all we had to do was push the buzzer and wait for the other to pick up. It was great! We could talk and not have to yell into the floor vent. The Stepmother must have had enough of our conversations. We didn't care, we had a phone, and we didn't feel so alone in our confinement.

Times were still hard though. The Stepmother was so mean all the time. For instance, she knew I had a gag reflex when it came to cooked canned spinach. I'd dry heave at the smell of the stuff. Oh, she loved to make a great big bowl of the slimy stuff and make me eat it until I puked. Every time I gagged, she'd slap me across the face, jamming another heaping spoonful into my mouth. I'm almost gagging just thinking about it! Tears, blood, puke, and slobber, and that nasty green slimy spinach. Yuck! My teeth were bloody from the spoon being jammed into my mouth. My nose was bleeding from the slaps and my head was pounding from it all.

That kind of stuff went on a lot after Sissy went to school. My dad was at work, Sissy was at school, and it was just The Stepmother and me alone with her hatred for me. She definitely had a hatred for me, and I didn't know why. It's not like I was a bad kid; I really wasn't. It's still so strange to me that she acted that way towards me.

At that age, I just knew she was mean, and I was scared of her. Times kind of got a little better after my little sister was born. The Stepmother was busy with a new baby now, and I was just in the way. So, most of the time, I was put in my room to play alone or pushed outside if the baby was sleeping. Keep in mind, I wasn't quite four years old at the time. Would you send a three-year-old outside to just wander around alone? No fence to keep me from the road, no one watching over me.

I can't imagine doing that nowadays.

6

The Little Shepherd

I was young, but I remember it very clearly. I loved being outside. I liked looking around the farm. There was a new feeding trough that hadn't been used yet that was sitting next to the big red barn. I'd climb into it on a cold day, and it was warm when the sun was out, heating up the metal. We had an AM radio that looked like Snoopy the Dog. I remember that somehow, I ended up with it outside and I took it into the trough with me. I turned it on, and the song Dream Weaver came on.

If you've heard the beginning of that song with the notes spinning off into the air, you'll know what I'm talking about. If not, set the book down, look it up, and give it a listen. Close your eyes and just listen to the notes being played. It's hard to explain how the music sounded in that metal feeding trough. The sounds seemed to be coming at me from all sides. It was like magic as the notes spun off into the air. Every time I hear that song it takes me back to that day. I know that's an odd thing to write about, but listening to the radio in that trough made me happy, and happy was a hard thing to find back then.

But on most days, when I was put outside, I would go out into the fields and find the sheep. There were hundreds of them, sheep everywhere, and I'd just follow them around.

I spent so much time with those sheep, I bet they thought I was a sheep too. If it was a sunny day, I'd try and find a big momma sheep sleeping in the sun. I'd slowly lay next to her and use her like a pillow, only to wake when she'd move on with the flock.

Once a year, a big group of shepherds would come to the farm. They were the Basque people. The Basque people are from a region in Spain near France. The Basques have a long history with sheep as shepherds and are known as sheep experts. There's even a sheep on their regional flag. That's how much sheep are valued to them.

This group of shepherds traveled around to big sheep farms, as needed, to shear the sheep's wool, trim their hooves, and look over the sheep's health. They'd give the sheep shots and de-worm them or whatever was needed. As a young boy, as you can imagine, I was in the middle of it all. I had my little staff and would move sheep from one place to another as directed.

The sheep knew me, so it actually really helped to keep them calm having me involved. One job I had was being a door, as it were, from the sheep pen to where the shepherds were working. I'd stand in the gap with my little staff across the doorway, only letting one sheep at a time through when the shepherds called for them. I can remember how quiet the sheep were as they waited for their turn to be called. They would just stand there quietly looking at me with those big brown eyes and black faces. It was like they were asking me "is it my turn yet?"

A few years ago, I was reading the Gospel of John for the first time. It's the passage where Jesus is saying He's the Good Shepherd and the gate to the sheepfold. The Good Shepherd will call the sheep out who are waiting there for him. From those early days on the farm, I knew exactly what John chapter 10 was talking about!

How a good shepherd loves his sheep and tends to all their needs, and what a gate to a "sheepfold" (or what we would call a sheep pen) really is. I was like, "Hey! I know what that is!" It's someone who's in the doorway to the pen controlling the sheep as they're waiting to be called out, waiting for the shepherd's call.

I've done that as a boy. I've been a gate like that, and I know what a good shepherd looks like. John 10 is my favorite chapter in the Bible because it reminds me of the time I spent with the sheep and those shepherds in my youth. Seeing how the shepherds really loved those sheep and were gentle with them, caring for their every need. Jesus says He's the Good Shepherd and we are His sheep. Trust me, that's a good thing. If you ever have a chance, go to a sheep farm, then read John 10 and Psalm 23. It will change how you read those verses forever.

The farmer that owned all the sheep that I was helping with was an old man named Mr. Kraft. He really liked me and was always super nice too. Maybe he was nice because he'd see me with the sheep all the time and how they took me in as one of the flock, or maybe because I couldn't pronounce my words that well yet. I just called him Mr. Crap. I know, right? At that time, I never understood why he'd laugh so hard when I'd say hi to him. "Hi, Mr. Crap," I'd say.

He'd laugh and say, "Hi kid! How are my sheep doing? Are you keeping an eye on them for me?"

"Yep!" I'd reply.

I followed him around the farm like a puppy, helping him with chores, chatting him up with a million questions. I bet I was more in the way than not, but I liked helping him and he didn't seem to mind. I was always a little sad when he had to go home. He'd say, "See ya kid! I got to go," jumping on his big green tractor. "Stay back now," he'd say, as he headed off across the field, back to his house on the horizon. That was always a highlight of my day, helping Mr. Kraft.

Another was when Sissy would get home from school. I hated being so alone all the time. I couldn't wait for Sissy to get home. When the school bus finally brought her home, I'd most often be waiting in the yard for her. "Sissy, let's play!" I'd say.

"I have to water the pigs first, then we can play," she'd tell me.

On this particular day, I said, "Let's play hide and go seek!"

"OK," she said. "You go hide and after I finish watering the pigs I'll come and look for you." I remember running all over the place looking for the perfect place to hide. Moving from this place to that, always watching to see if she'd finished yet and was on the hunt for me. My dad had an old pickup with an even older camper on the back of it.

"This is perfect, she'll never find me in there!" I thought, "Sissy doesn't like the old camper…" I snuck in through the door looking for the perfect spot to hide.

The cabinets were too high and too small. The bunk was too open. At the bottom of the cabinets there was a little icebox type of refrigerator. It was small, but I was able to back into it scrunching my knees tight to my chest…CLICK.

I remember that sound as the door locked with me inside. It was dark and I realized I didn't like that spot after all. I pushed on the door thinking it would just open, but it didn't. I pushed as hard as I could, and nothing happened. Panicked, I started yelling for Sissy. I remember hitting the door with my hands and yelling for what felt like forever.

It was getting so hot in there and I was starting to get sleepy and short of breath. I remember a feeling of fear, instinctively knowing this was bad. "SISSY! SISSY! SISSY! Help me!" I yelled. "SISSY! SISSY! SISSY!" over and over again.

That was the first time I felt like Death was there with me, and only a moment away from taking me. It was so scary being trapped in the darkness with no hope...then, CLICK! The door opened and Sissy was there! She said, "What are you doing in there?"

I can still feel the cool air rushing in, as I struggled to get a breath. I asked how she found me. "I don't know...I just did," she said.

Now looking back, I think this was one of those times when God can be seen in my story. He didn't show himself in a big way with a voice leading my sister to help. No, I think He just guided my sister to me, without her knowing why.

That old camper was scary, and my sister didn't like it, that's why I chose it for a hiding spot. She would never look in there. Yet she did. And she didn't know why. So many kids have died in old refrigerators over the years. That's why they had to change the design. Why was I spared? I didn't know. All I knew was, don't tell Dad what had just happened. We agreed, and I never went into that camper again.

I still get a little claustrophobic, even to this day.

7

The Last Christmas

By now, I was five years old and soon it would be Christmas. Sissy and I loved listening to the old Cinnamon Bear radio program as we laid in front of the giant old radio console cabinet. Christmas meant a call from my grandparents who lived in California (my real mom's dad and his wife.) Oddly, my dad had contacted them after he and my mom got the divorce. I liked talking to them at Christmas. They were really nice and always sent me nice presents, Matchbox cars and candy. But most of all, Christmas meant a visit from my mom.

We didn't get to see her very often, once or twice a year. I was so happy! Mom was coming to see us. Maybe we could go with her this time. I remember looking out the window, straining my eyes at every car that passed, hoping to see her pulling into our driveway.

"Get away from that window!" The Stepmother yelled at me. I snuck into my room with the lights out and peaked through my window hoping to see my mom drive up. Finally, she did.

"MOM'S HERE!" I yelled, running for the door. I was all cleaned up with my hair slicked back. I had washed my face and was so careful not to spill on my shirt while eating dinner. I wanted to look my best for her. Nothing that would make her not want me this time.

I heard her knocking. My dad opened the door and there she was: Mom. I rushed forward, wrapping myself around her legs, almost tripping her in my embrace. "Get back!" my dad scolded me. But I couldn't contain my joy, Mom was here, and I didn't care what anyone said.

We sat on the couch. I'm sure Sissy and I talked a hundred miles an hour as we told her all about everything we had done since the last time we'd seen her. My dad reluctantly took a photo of us with my mom's camera as we sat next to each other on the couch. I remember the gift she brought me that Christmas. It looked like a round suitcase, but when you opened it, it was the bridge of the Starship Enterprise from Star Trek. It came with all the action figures too: Captain Kirk, Spock, the Doctor, and others. I wish I still had it; it was great! She helped me get it all set up, as we sat on the floor.

My dad and The Stepmother just sat there at the kitchen table saying nothing, awkwardly watching over everything. I noticed but didn't care. Nothing was going to spoil this moment. We played and talked. It was wonderful!

Then my dad barked, "TIME'S UP, TIME TO GO!"

"NO!" I cried. "Not yet. PLEASE! Just a little longer!"

My mom looked heartbroken at my tears. "I have a long drive back home," she tried to tell me, looking for an excuse to comfort me. I remember my dad and The Stepmother saying a few coarse words to my mom as she got on her coat. My mom looked so sad as she hugged Sissy and I goodbye.

I remember thinking, "Why can't I go with her this time? Maybe I was bad and talked too much? Maybe I shouldn't have hugged her so hard when she got there? Yes, that had to be it! My dad yelled at me, and I almost tripped her. She must be mad at me. I have to be better next time! I can't talk so much and hug her so hard!" my little mind was scolding myself. I can still feel the guilt I'd imposed on myself as I write these words, all these years later.

I was sad and crying. Just moments after the door shut, there was a hard thud to the side of my head. The Stepmother had hit me. "I'll give you something to cry about!" she yelled. She liked to hit me in the head and grab my sister by the hair jerking her back and forth. She gave us both a good beating because we had shown my mom too much affection. I was already feeling bad about my mom not wanting me. It hurt and I cried, but in my little mind, the beating was something I deserved.

Years later, my mom told me that she stood outside the door sobbing as she heard us getting beat because of her. She said she wanted to get in the car and drive it through the house killing us all, so we didn't have to suffer anymore. That's when she decided not to come around anymore. If her kids were suffering because of her, she couldn't do that to us again, she thought.

And just like that, my mom was gone…again.

I've carried guilt for most of my life that I was the cause of my mom not returning after that day. She didn't call, she never came around. It was like she had vanished. I'd sometimes punch myself when I'd feel the guilt of it. I don't know why I would. Maybe, if I was punished enough or sorry enough for showing my mom too much affection, she'd return. I know now, I wasn't the cause, but I've struggled letting the feeling of guilt go. It's even affected the way I show affection to my wife. I struggle to show her I love her and it's even harder to tell her that I do.

I'm working on it. I hope writing this book will help me to let go of the things I'm writing about, and the things I'm leaving out as well. A place for it to live outside of me. A place I can put on a shelf and hope to forget about most of it.

Life went on with too many bad days to write about. When I was almost seven years old, we moved from the farm to a house that was out in the woods. Our new house was about a half of a mile down a long gravel road. The road was an old train line with its tracks removed. It was a little spooky, since the road grade had been cut out of the landscape to make it flat, and the trees had grown up and over it like a tunnel. It might remind you of something from the Headless Horseman story, with the trees looking like they could reach down and grab you at any moment.

Our house was tucked way back into an area of large trees. It was dark and nothing like the farm. I was scared of the dark and my dad liked to tease me that Bigfoot was out there in the woods. That freaked me out! Our house was a ranch style house with a two-car garage that had been converted into a laundry room, a small bathroom, and one very small room that was almost a large closet.

That's where my room was to be. Out in the small room, at the other end of the house, in the garage. A room without curtains on the window. I was so sure Bigfoot was going to look through the window and see me sleeping, break the glass, grab me, and drag me into the woods to my death. I was so scared.

I'd sleep with my back as tight to the wall as I could, hoping Bigfoot wouldn't see me there. If he did, no one would hear me scream because they were all at the other end of the house and there was a door to the house from the garage that they always kept closed to keep the house from getting cold. I was doomed. Bigfoot was definitely going to get me; it was only a matter of time.

My room had a concrete floor with an old throw rug on it and it was very cold in the winter. My bed was a stack of old mattresses that touched both walls. If I sat on the floor with my back to the bed, I could almost touch the other wall where a cabinet had been built-in next to the back of the fireplace brickwork. It was a very small room. We had a cat named Fido that I'd have sleep with me to help with the mice in my room. Mice liked to run through my room at night and it freaked me out when they'd get on my bed.

There was a small field on the other side of the house, that was only about a half-acre in size. It was full of old stumps and brush, but my dad always had a fire burning, and eventually there was enough grass to get a sheep. I was glad that we were getting a sheep, I missed my old friends from the farm. It was spring, and we didn't have a barn, and the sheep was still a baby lamb, so where do you think they put the sheep? Yep, out in the garage with me. Mice, sheep poop, Bigfoot, The Stepmother. Ugh! What an existence.

After moving to the new house, life started to spiral downward. My dad and The Stepmother were fighting all the time. My dad started to drink until he passed out most nights. The Stepmother was always drinking, either whiskey and RC Cola or wine by the gallon. Her hate for me was getting more and more out in the open. I had to keep out of the way, and I also developed a flinch from getting smacked around all the time. If you moved near me, I'd flinch. I couldn't help it. It made me a target at school as well. The kids thought it was funny to make me flinch by moving quickly near me. You'd think the teachers would have noticed a kid with bruises and a flinch. You would think they would start asking questions or report it to the authorities. But sadly, they never did, as far as I know.

But God had a plan for my life it seems. His plan was to have me stay where I was, and it took me into the darkness. God's plan had to have darkness in it, darkness to shine His light into.

The picture taken at the last Christmas

8

◆

Fight or Die

In my next memory I'm going to share, it was almost Mother's Day, and I was seven years old. My dad loaded me and both my sisters into the car, and we drove to town. We parked behind a building, and he told us to get out. We went in through a door and there sat my mom...I was in shock! What was she doing here? She didn't look very happy to see us.

I was upset that my little sister was there. It wasn't her mom, why was she even there? And my dad seemed to be pushing her onto my mom, taking all of the time away from me. She and my dad started arguing. The tension was thick in the air. We didn't stay long, and it was very confusing. My mom didn't really talk to me, and I thought it was because of before. She still must be mad at me, I thought. We left, my dad was so mad, and I didn't know why.

A few days later, my dad and The Stepmother told me and Sissy we had to call our mom and tell her we never wanted to see her again. It was Mother's Day, of all days.

I said "No," then SMACK! A blow upside my head.

"Do it!" they yelled.

"No!" SMACK! Another hit.

"Do it!" they yelled again.

"WHY?" I yelled.

"Because of the church!" they yelled.

"What?" I was confused.

They said because of church rules, it would ruin my life if my mom was in it. Their excuse was that if I was ever going to have a friend, since my mom wasn't in the church, no one would be around me.

Little did I know it was very odd that I didn't have any friends. Remember if you go to that church, you can't have friends outside of the church. No friends from the world were the rules. I didn't have a friend from the world or from the church. I'd only gone over to one boys house a couple of times because our dads were friends.

Typically, at Followers, it's the mom's job to make sure their kids are together from a young age. We didn't go to church that often and I didn't know anyone. The Stepmother didn't want me to have a friend, so she kept me isolated.

Nevertheless, I had to call my mom and tell her to never come around again. This was so hard for me to do. I already carried the guilt from a couple of years ago when she stopped coming to see us. A few days earlier she seemed to still be upset with me and now I was going to tell her to stay away.

My dad picked up the phone and dialed it. My mom answered and he said that I had something to tell her. I said, "Mom… I don't want you to come around anymore because of the church rules." It was a really odd thing to say because I hadn't seen her for a couple of years already.

I just knew she was going to tell me off and say something mean, but she didn't. In her soft voice she said, "It's OK… I know they're making you say that. I wouldn't want to ruin your life. I'll stay away."

And that was it. My dad took the phone from me, yelled something at her, and then hung it up. It was so confusing to me. Why was this happening? My dad was so angry, and The Stepmother was all fired up too.

The lump that's in my throat right now as I write this... how could they have done this to me? Why did they make me do that, especially on Mother's Day?

I didn't know then, but I do know now. My mom was getting remarried that day and it really made my dad mad that she was moving on. He always considered her as his property, and we were the leverage that he used to keep her under his control. Remember, he's a narcissist. He wanted to punish her. She was getting married to a good guy and my dad wasn't having it. That's why he took us to visit her, to put pressure on her.

It's so odd if you think about it. He'd gotten remarried. And it wasn't like he was sneaking over to see her; she wanted nothing to do with him besides to see her children. Just another layer of crazy. After that day they told me my mom had moved to Texas. That was a lie. She lived less than an hour away.

I guess after that day, knowing my mom was totally out of the picture, it opened the flood gates for the abuse to move into a new and horrifying direction. Something changed and I was now under attack. If I was happy, I had all sugar taken away from me for weeks. If I whistled, The Stepmother would punch me in the mouth. Yes, punch, not slap. Sometimes I would see it coming, but most of the time, I didn't see it coming.

My dad thought I should know how to hit and how to be hit. I thought the "how to be hit" was ironic because The Stepmother hit me all the time. My dad would get all liquored up and use me as a punching bag. Once, he hit me so hard I fell back through a wooden rocking chair. It knocked the wind out of me and left me bruised, front and back.

For the next two years, life was hard and so confusing for me. I was under an enormous amount of pressure all the time. I had to try and read their minds about what I should be doing, without knowing what it was, while working as a slave for a drunken hate-filled master. It was a dance of being seen, but not heard, and also being invisible at the same time.

I was now nine years old, and my life was filled with constant chores. I was like a live-in servant, with no time just to be a kid. It was my job to do all the outside chores, like feed and water the chickens and pigs, as well as mow the yard and pull weeds, regardless of the weather conditions. One of my most hated outside chores was untangling the goats from the blackberry vines they were tethered near. When I was finished with all the outside chores that I had to do, I had the inside chores to do as well.

The Stepmother would have me do all kinds of odd chores, filling every minute that I wasn't at school. I often had to mop the kitchen ceiling. I was made to climb under the house to remove all the spiderwebs. All kinds of really strange things like that, as well as normal housework, such as folding the clothes and doing the dishes after dinner. The Stepmother saved all the leftovers in old margarine containers. If she could scrape a spoonful out of the pot, after I put the leftovers in the tub, she'd make me eat it. I think I scraped the finish off of all the pots and pans in our kitchen, just to not have that spoon jammed into my mouth with a twist, hitting my tonsils and almost breaking my teeth. I'd vacuum and mop and clean the bathrooms. Everything had to be perfect.

This day that I'm going to share about was a day of endless chores. Remember, I was nine years old. The Stepmother called me into the hall bathroom. She had been in an extra grumpy mood that day. I heard her yelling for me and went to see what I'd done wrong this time. She was standing over the toilet with the seat up. I had cleaned the bathroom already and was wondering what I had missed.

She said, "Look at this!"

"What did I miss?" I asked, moving to look into the toilet.

She said, "Look at that!"

"What?" I asked.

She then grabbed me by the back of the neck and forced me towards the toilet bowl. She pushed me down to my knees and right over the bowl.

"LOOK AT THAT!" she yelled. "THAT IS NOT ACCEPTABLE!"

"What?" I asked. What was wrong? Evidently, I hadn't cleaned the toilet good enough. She pushed my face down into the bowl.

"LOOK AT THE MESS YOU LEFT!"

I couldn't see anything. I said, "I'm sorry, I'll fix it." She then did something I didn't see coming.

She said, "You're darn right you'll clean it again," as she forced my head into the water and started scrubbing the bowl with my face. My face was under water and being battered against the bowl's edges. I tried to lift my head, but she wasn't letting me. I was running out of air and pushed as hard as I could to lift my head out of the water. I pushed and she pushed back harder. She was trying to drown me in the toilet. I was fighting back with everything I had.

I'd get just a gulp of air and back into the water I'd go. Again, with the bashing around the bowl. My face was aching, and I was bleeding from my eyebrow. It had been split open; the water was now all bloody. I remember straining so hard, fighting for my life. But I also was thinking, "I should just let her kill me."

I was done with the beatings and constant mental abuse…her constantly telling me how worthless I was.

"Just kill me," I thought. But then, I thought how happy it would make her if she did, and I didn't want to give her the pleasure of being the one who did me in. If anyone was going to kill me, I'd do it myself.

I again pushed with all my strength. Gulp a little air and back I'd go. I was losing the battle. Remember, I was only a little kid against an overweight woman. She had the weight advantage and was almost standing over me as she pushed on my head with her upper weight while simultaneously kneeing me in the hip and ribs. I was just about to give up when I heard a voice in my head say, "FIGHT!" That's all. Just, "FIGHT!"

The toilet was in a corner and there was a small window up in the wall to my left. I remember thinking there was someone saying "Fight!" from that window.

So, I fought.

Again, I pushed my face out of the water. I pushed so hard it blew all the blood vessels out in the right side of my face and neck, down to my shoulder. It looked like someone had drawn spider webs in ink all over those areas. You could see where every vein ran. It looked like tattooed dark lines that resembled tree branches from my ear through my neck area, and down to my right shoulder,

I remember looking into the bloody water as the blood continued gushing from my eyebrow thinking, "I have to flush the water out or next time I won't have the energy to lift my face out for air." I had to make a choice. Drown? Or take the bash of letting my arm go so I could flush the toilet. I braced myself for the blow, as she was putting all her weight on my neck and head and kneeing me in the side.

I moved as fast as I could with my left hand and flushed the toilet. That left only my right arm to hold back her force, and that wasn't enough. Smash! My face hit the toilet bowl with a thud. I could breathe for a few seconds, but the water in the bowl was filling again. It's a horrible feeling having bloody water slowly cover your face as someone is trying to drown you in it.

I forced my face out of the water again and reached for the flusher handle. Thud. That was my head smashing into the bowl again. I tried to reach the handle when I was face down in there but couldn't reach it. I only had a little more fight left in me. She was not giving up and I wasn't either. It was like she'd went crazy with hate for me. Where was she getting the energy to keep this up?

It was somewhere between five to ten minutes that we were fighting, but it felt like an eternity. Then it popped into my head to just reach back behind the toilet and turn off the water. So, I started reaching and found a knob. I turned it and the water that was filling the toilet turned off. I don't know how I knew how to do that. I was a little kid and knew nothing about toilets.

She finally just let me go with a shove. She was beside herself with rage. She had lost the fight; I was still alive. I can't really explain how scary the whole thing was. It was horrible! I just sat there on the floor gasping for air as the blood ran down my face. My eye was starting to swell shut and my lip was starting to swell too. My head was pounding, and my ribs hurt where she'd been kneeing me. The adrenaline was pumping through my veins. With every beat of my heart, it felt like my hair was sticking straight out with the rhythm and it made me feel sick. What had just happened? She had just tried to kill me. This was new—she'd beat me without stopping lots of times, but this was new. The hate she had for me. Why? What had I done?

I think this is another place you can see God in my story. Fight and turn off the water. Without those prompts in my mind, I don't know if I would have survived. I grabbed a handful of toilet paper and put it on my eyebrow to try and stop the bleeding as I ran for the woods to hide.

This wasn't the first time I'd gone out into the vast woods that surrounded our home to hide. I knew the trails and my parents didn't. I could outrun them and out hide them too. They would never find me if I needed to hide. It was scary though, being out there where the Bigfoot might get me, but being where The Stepmother was actually trying to kill me was much scarier.

I remember having to hide out in the woods and being so scared. I remembered a couple of hymns we would sing sometimes at church that gave me comfort. We didn't go to church that often, but for some reason these hymns stuck with me. 'Onward Christian Soldiers' when I needed to be brave, and 'Jesus Is All the World to

Me' when I was sad. Both were odd because I didn't really know who Jesus was. And I didn't know all the words, but I would sing them out loud the best I could.

Jesus is all the world to me,
my life, my joy, my all.
He is my strength from day to day,
without Him I would fall:
When I am sad, to Him I go,
No other one can cheer me so;
When I am sad, He makes me glad,
He's my friend.

It gave me comfort, like I wasn't all alone, like singing those words would somehow protect me from my fears. And you know what? It did. God was watching over me during those times of fear and pain. I didn't know Jesus then, but He knew me.

After this attack, The Stepmother made up a lie about me back-talking her or something. All my dad said to me was, "You need to do what you're told next time without any back talk!"

They kept me out of school until the lines in my neck weren't so noticeable. I knew after that day that my dad didn't have my back, and The Stepmother was out to get me. I had to be on my toes all the time now if I were to survive.

Things with Sissy started to change too. She was really quiet all the time and hid in her room "doing homework." She started to be mean to me as well. We would argue all the time and it was like she started to blame me for all the problems in the house. She was falling into the trap of lies. The Stepmother was almost as mean to Sissy as she was to me and I think it broke her, but the Little Sister could do no wrong. She was The Stepmother's daughter and protected. Nevertheless, the house was a war zone.

During that time, when I was around nine years old, Sissy changed from my friend and protector to my Older Sister, my enemy. Sissy was gone. She wasn't happy anymore and she would hardly talk to me. It broke my heart. I was now totally alone in a house of horrors where I was the enemy to everyone.

The Stepmother thought it was fun to have the Sisters attack me. They'd run in from another room and start punching me and kicking me. I had to fight them both at the same time. I'd grab the Little Sister by the hair and try and knock her down while fending off blows from the Older Sister. We started fighting like this now and then, and it went on for years. The only thing that stopped it, I think, was when I started to grow stronger as a teenager. They just couldn't hit as hard as I could.

It began to be a spectator sport. My dad and The Stepmother would get all liquored up and sit in their chairs cheering us on as we duked it out. When I started to win, The Stepmother would sometimes get in the fray with us and I had to fight her as well, alongside The Sisters. They'd tackle me, pinning me down as The Stepmother would punch me in the face. It was absolutely crazy! She knew how to hit and with my head pinned to the floor the impact of the punch was devastating. It actually stopped The Sisters once from attacking me, when The Stepmother was punching me so hard. They told her to stop. It was even too much for them to watch.

I'd typically freak out with rage after an attack. I'd be yelling at everyone, swinging at whatever moved as I tried to reach the door for an escape. My dad would just sit there and laugh at me or spring to his feet and say, "You think you're tough?" as he entered the battle too. My only rescue was getting to a door and running for the woods. Sometimes I'd make it… and sometimes I wouldn't. You can only be punched and kicked so many times before you'll actually pee blood for a couple of days. I'm not a doctor, but I don't think that's a good sign when that happens.

I'm sorry, reader, if this is too much. I'm sorry, but it's actually the tip of the iceberg. It's going to get darker. This next bit is hard to revisit. It's all going to happen in a six-year time span. I thought life was bad before…

I'm not sure people realize how much your childhood makes you who you are as an adult. How, if you're loved and nurtured by a caring adult when you're young, most people turn out "normal", well, as normal as you might seem to the world around you, but normal, nevertheless. Growing up without loving parents really affects how you see the world and how the world sees you.

For me, I was isolated. I was told so many lies that I was worthless. I was told people didn't like me, just because I was me. After a while, I believed it, and why wouldn't I? It didn't help that I didn't really understand how people interacted with each other. This has been very difficult for me most of my life, and I think it's made me a little different. I'm older now and it's much easier to blend in with the group, but I bet if you asked people that know me, they'd say I'm just a little bit different.

It seemed everyone was speaking a different language—the language of social skills. You know…how people interact with each other and why. It's a very hard language to learn when you're older. I've learned the language better now, but just like someone who speaks English but spoke something other before, they'll have an accent of the language they first spoke. Not growing up knowing how normal people interact, I have an accent, as it were, an accent that unfortunately causes me sometimes to get it wrong. Social skills are difficult even if you were raised normal, that's why most of my life, I was very quiet when in crowds. Really, really quiet. Most of the time I was just observing everyone, trying to learn why they acted the way they do. Why are some people funny? Why are some people so popular when they're actually jerks to everyone?

The hardest thing for me to learn was conversation. I have really worked on this, and I think I do all right now, especially If I've never met you. It's much easier for me, if I don't know you, to talk to you. I can chat it up like the best of them, but it's been really hard and taken years of study to do so. My wife tells me it's because I was never taught how to interact with peers from a young age. That's typically what the mother teaches you: how to… I don't know… be normal like everyone else. I think that teaching, along with how you're programmed as a child, it all makes a difference on how you act when you're an adult as well.

It didn't help that I was constantly told lies:

"You're bad."

"You're worthless."

"It'd be best for everyone if you just died."

"You'll never amount to anything."

"You're a liar and basically a bad person, just like your mother."

That last one really bothered me when they'd say that to me. I *was* not and I *am* not a liar! And, I didn't know my mother, so why do you say that about her to me? I remember when we'd meet someone for the first time, The Stepmother would introduce me, and the very next thing she'd say was, "He's a liar, you can't believe anything he says!"

The way people would look at me was so horrible to endure. I now wonder if they'd think, "that's an odd thing to say about a child just after meeting them." I wonder if they'd look at me oddly thinking, "OK, what's the parent trying to hide that the kid might say?" I don't know, but at the time, it was horrible.

The Sisters and I were fighting all the time, they'd tell me how much they both hated me. I had trouble making friends at church. Most of the kids at school were really mean to me, too. I spent most of my time alone. So, as you can imagine, my mental state was starting to be compromised.

I was being crushed under the world I was stuck in.

9

The Buckle

One day, a few months later, me and my sisters were home alone. We were arguing about something, and it was getting heated. The Older Sister was going to call The Stepmother and tell on me because I wouldn't do everything she said. She had turned into a tyrant, and I was her slave. The Little Sister was a brat most of the time and knew she could get away with murder because her mom was The Stepmother. We seemed to fight and argue with every word we spoke to one another. The Stepmother's evil manipulation of us, along with the fist fights, had made the Sisters and me enemies.

We were in the kitchen and the Older Sister had the phone in her hand. We were yelling at each other. I turned my head to yell at the Little Sister. That's when it happened. Bang! My head was spinning. The Older Sister threw the phone at me hitting me on the side of the head. Remember this wasn't a cell phone. It was one of those 1970's style phones. Big and heavy. It knocked me to the ground. When I got up, I called her a name I shouldn't have. I was yelling at her and then her face changed as she looked over my shoulder. I spun around thinking the Little Sister was on the attack from behind. But to my surprise it was my dad standing there.

He looked crazy in his eyes. I'm sure he'd been drinking. What was he doing home at that time of day? He was taking off his belt and winding the belt end around his hand, leaving about fifteen inches with the buckle hanging from his hand. "Oh no..." I thought.

The buckle…

My dad worked for the Miller Brewing Company delivering beer to stores. The buckle was a prize he'd won from work. It was about four inches long and three inches wide and made of solid brass. It had a raised shape of the Miller logo on the front. It was a weapon, and he was getting ready to hit me with it. He was fat and drunk, but I was small and fast. That was my only defense.

"RUN!" I thought.

I took off as he made his first swing, barely missing my head as I ducked it to the left. I'd acted like I was going to go to the right, so he was already throwing his weight that way, but I sidestepped him to the left and headed for the living room door. He spun around quicker than I thought he could and was in pursuit. I knew I couldn't make it out the front door without him catching me, so I thought I'd run towards the hallway and make a quick turn back into the kitchen and head for the back door. I had to get out of the house and into the woods.

The kitchen had a doorway from the hall and also to the living room, so if I could make the loop and out turn him, I could get away. As I made my turn for the hallway, I glanced at the square mirrors that we had glued to a living room wall (this was a fad that people did in the 1970's). As I glanced, I noticed how close my dad was, he was only about half of a swing away. I again ducked and SMASH! A bunch of mirrors broke into pieces. I had dodged another attack.

The only problem was I'd missed my turn into the kitchen and was committed to the hallway now. This limited my escape routes. Maybe I could make it to a bedroom and get out a window. That would only work if I was able to slam the door in his face and slow him down for a few seconds. Even if that worked, the likelihood of me making it out a window was slim.

I turned up the speed, but so had he, and with the extra reach of the belt and extra rage from the smashed mirrors fueling his anger; he had me. Thud! The first blow from the buckle hit me on my right shoulder. My right arm went limp, it felt like it was broken. I'd reached the end of the hallway and with a limp arm I had no chance to get out a window. The best thing I could do was turn and face him and fight. I spun around and he was already in the motion of striking me again. I raised my left arm to block the blow as he swung down from above. Thud! It hit with enough force to force my arm down as it struck the top meaty area of my forearm. He swung again, and again I used my arm to block the blow. This one hit the underneath part of my left arm near my elbow. Oh, it hurt so bad, but I had to protect my head.

As he was getting ready to hit me again, I started opening the door to the closet that was at the end of the hallway behind me. The closet had shelves in it that held extra blankets and board games. The bottom of the closet had shelves about three feet from the floor for bigger things. With my limp right arm, I started grabbing whatever was in there and dragging it out to make room for me to possibly squeeze into that space and find shelter from the attack. Thud! He hit me again. Again, to the top part of my forearm. He was cussing at me and acting like he was out of his mind. I don't know what or how long he'd been drinking, but he was out of his head.

I quickly crouched down and squeezed myself into the closet as he hit me again. Thud! This time it was my shin as I pulled my legs up to my chest trying to be as small as possible. My leg felt like it was broken. He swung again and I turned just in time to take the hit to the meatier part of my leg.

I was screaming at him to stop. "PLEASE STOP!" He hit me again, my right forearm this time took the hit just below the wrist. That arm was now useless. "STOP DAD! STOP!"

He staggered in his drunkenness and kicked at me as I squeezed myself as deep into the closet as I could, grabbing anything I could to use to block the blows. He was breathing heavy and having to stop the cussing rant to catch his breath. He staggered back a few steps and went into the bathroom to his right. That was my opportunity to escape. I took it and crawled out of the closet. My arm was still limp, and my leg almost wouldn't work, but fear will push you past the pain. And a push is what I needed right then. I was only nine years old, but I was smart enough to run when I had the chance.

Out the back door I limped. I had to make it into the woods. I had to hide. It was cold outside as I crawled into a low spot under some brush, my body shaking with the pain. The cold ground felt good on my injuries. I pulled some brush up over me to try and get warm, as well as to help with my camouflage, just in case they came looking for me. I laid as still as I could, trying to stop the shivering as to not give away my location. My body ached. I was in so much pain, but worse, my heart was broken.

This time I stayed out there until way after dark. They yelled my name and blew a whistle for me to come home, but I wasn't going to go back. Not until the lights were out and I could sneak back into my room.

I'd taken a lot of beatings from him before, but nothing like this.

Things had changed, just like the toilet incident that had happened just a few months before. I truly think my dad would have killed me. I don't think he wanted to, not like The Stepmother did, but I think in his drunken rage he would have done it, not knowing that he had.

The day after the attack, I was yelled at for making him so mad. I deserved it, they said, for the broken mirrors and using the cuss word against my sister. I wanted to say, "You were yelling way worse cuss words at me while you were beating me," but I kept my mouth shut. The bruises on my arms were so deep and large, you could actually see the shape of the raised part on the buckle and the Miller Brewing Company logo backwards in my skin. I had to wear long sleeve shirts for weeks to hide the bruises. I think my shoulder was probably cracked along with my shin bone, both turned black and hurt to the touch, but luckily, I was able to use them normally after a few weeks of pain.

I was told to say, "I fell out of a tree," if anyone asked.

10

A Cry For The Snow To Save Me

After that day, I wanted to die. I couldn't take anymore. I thought about running away, but then I thought, they would just find me, and I'd get beat again. No, I was done. I started to plan how I was going to end my life. I thought of every way I could imagine doing it, and the pros and cons to each. It had to be soon before I changed my mind, but I had a concern: Hell.

We didn't go to church much, like I'd said before, but I'd heard that if you kill yourself, you'd go to Hell. I wasn't even sure God was real, so Hell might not be real either. I wrestled with it for days. I didn't know what to do. Just kill myself and wait and see, or I didn't know... What should I do?

I couldn't talk to anyone with the question of "if you kill yourself where would you go?" That would screw everything up. The authorities would take me out of the church, and I was taught that was the ultimate thing to fear. I only had one thing left to do: Pray.

God works in mysterious ways in our lives. How He works in your life probably looks totally different than everyone else's lives around you. How He moves you, how He comforts you, and how He shows you He's real. For me I had a little of all these things. The comfort of the hymns I would sing when in the woods so alone and scared. How He put in my head to "FIGHT!" when I was about to give up while being drowned in the toilet. But this time He did something that some might find hard to believe. It's OK if you don't believe me. I know it happened, and it doesn't really matter if you believe me or not.

But I can prove it did happen. How? I'm not dead.

Remember, I was nine years old and had hardly gone to church. My dad shook a Bible at me once, but I'd never read one. I knew of a person called God who lived in heaven. But I'd just found out that Santa Claus wasn't real. Was God real? Who was He and why would He care about me? I thought He's just like Santa Claus, a fairytale. I wanted Him to not be real in my heart, because if He was real, I couldn't kill myself. If He was real, I'd either have to stay here in a living Hell or die and go there. I'd never prayed before. What do I say? How do I do it? I'd seen a yard statue of a person on their knees with their hands together praying. Maybe that's what you do? So, I did.

I started the prayer with, "God, I've never prayed before. I don't know if you're real. I want to die, and I don't know if I can, without going to Hell. If you're real, show me you are, and I won't kill myself. And if you're not real, it won't matter."

It was a Sunday when I prayed, and it was supposed to snow that night. We were hoping it would, so we didn't have to go to school. So, in my prayer, I asked God to answer in a very specific way. I prayed, "God, if you are real, I want it to snow 1 foot deep in my yard. I want it to last 5 days, and I want to have 4 days off of school. If that doesn't happen, then you're not real, and I'm doing it."

The next morning, I woke up with the Little Sister running into my room saying, "IT SNOWED! IT SNOWED A LOT! AND WE

DON'T HAVE TO GO TO SCHOOL!"

I sat up and thought, "It snowed? A LOT?!" I went to the box with all the pencils in it and found a wooden ruler. I walked out the back door and, oh my goodness, there was a lot of snow. More than I ever remember seeing in our yard. I knelt down and pushed the ruler in. It slid in until my finger touched the snow. It was a foot deep in my yard. I looked up and thought, "Could it be real? No school today... I wonder." Time will tell.

With each day watching the news and them saying "No school tomorrow," I started to believe that God just might be real. We had 4 days off of school and on the 5th day the snow melted away.

"GOD IS REAL!" I couldn't believe He was.

Why did He answer the prayer of a little boy who never really knew Him? Only God can answer that question. Psalm 34:17-18 says, "When the righteous cry for help, the Lord hears and delivers them out of all their troubles. The Lord is near to the brokenhearted and saves the crushed in spirit."

In no way do I think that I was "the righteous," but I think God loves little children, and cares. He hears you when you cry out to Him when you're crushed, broken, and without hope. I was all of those things, and I needed him desperately. What I did know, from that moment on, was God is real!

I needed to know this, because the next six years would be even worse than the first nine.

I now knew God was real, but I still didn't know who Jesus was. He chose to show Himself to me much later in the story.

11

◆

White Hats and Flying Monkeys

Sometimes I was so cold in my bedroom that I would sneak into the living room as the sun was coming up and lay on the floor in the sunshine. I'd lay there trying to warm up in the sun, as it shone through the front window. I'd watch the dust as it swirled around in the morning rays. It was peaceful and quiet.

I would often wonder what my mom was doing. What adventures was she having in Texas? Did she have horses? Was there cactus where she lived, like in those old western movies? Did she ever think about me? Had she forgiven me? I never heard from her or got a birthday card or anything from her since that day I'd told her to stay away. I must have really done it, telling her to never talk to me again. I'd think about the "What if's."

What if I'd went with her to Texas? Would I be a cowboy and ride the range? Would she help me to figure out how to not be worthless? I saw the movie *The Wizard of OZ* on the TV and would dream that I was swept off into that world for a grand adventure, my mom being Glinda The Good Witch would save me from the Evil Stepmother and her flying monkeys. We'd live far away from anything that might hurt us.

If I heard anyone stirring in the morning hours, I'd sneak back to my place in the garage, trying to remember where I was on the adventure as I crawled back into my cold bed.

Time slowly marched on with some quiet days, and some days of total chaos. I was growing up, and luckily my parents found a few friends at the church who had kids around my age. Because of this, I made a couple of friends too. I had lived so long without any friends it was odd to have interaction in this way.

There were kids at school that I played with at recess, but I couldn't be real friends with them because of the church rules. Being nine or ten years old before I'd had a friend at the church was really weird.

When we did go to church, I remember walking around and seeing large groups of boys and girls talking to each other. I thought they must be cousins or something, why else would they know each other? I didn't understand that all the kids knowing each other was normal at the church. Kids knew each other from a very young age. The moms would make sure of it.

That never happened for me. I was never around them and didn't have a clue that I was supposed to be. It was all very confusing to me. I was a sophomore in high school before I figured out why all the kids knew each other. When I did go to church, even at such a young age, I was totally ignored or picked on by the other kids, that made me just stay in the shadows and never talk with anyone.

I'd mentioned before in the story that we didn't go to church that often. My dad never really fit in with the group after coming into the church. I think he believed that his only chance of going to heaven was to be a part of that church, but he never really fit in with the crowd. He was rough in the way he spoke. He liked to use foul language and tell raunchy jokes. He was a drunk and a womanizer, and people steered clear of him, but we were considered to be a part of the church anyway. He just didn't make going to church a priority. I think it would be months between us going to church or not.

I doubt The Stepmother fit in very well out at the church either because she had a rough and bold personality. These days calling her a Karen would be putting it mildly. I once saw her get in a man's face and yell at him because he was smoking. My dad smoked all the time, and it wasn't a big deal to him, but she liked to be the boss of everyone and if anything bothered her, she felt entitled to get in your face and tell you off. That man told my dad to tell her to get out of his face before he punched her in the mouth and then punched my dad in the mouth for letting her talk to him like that. My dad shrugged his shoulders and said, "Go ahead and hit her, I don't care."

Since The Stepmother was my mortal enemy, I was thinking, "Oh ya, she's going to get it now!" but sadly the guy just stomped off. I hope that gives you, the reader, an insight as to why we weren't at church that much when I was young.

After getting a few friends out at the church, my parents tried to go to church a little bit more. That was great for me because once in a while one of my new friends would call and see if I could go to their house after church to play. This was exciting, albeit a little strange. I could go to their houses, but they usually couldn't come to my house. I didn't care because any time away from my house was a much-needed rest from the crazy. But why couldn't they come to my house, you might ask?

Well...my parents had started to have big parties at our house, and I don't think it was a secret as to what was going on. Oddly, at their parties, I was left to just be there, as long as I stayed out of the way. I've often wondered why they did that. I have since come to the conclusion that it's like being a servant to a powerful person. The servant probably sees, and hears, and knows more of what's actually going on behind the scenes. They probably know more than the closest advisor because the servant sees everything. The servant is invisible to the powerful person, and it doesn't really matter what they see or hear because the servant is beneath them, and of no consequence. I think I was a servant to them in their eyes.

So, during these parties, I would stay out of the way and just observe. I'd see all kinds of crazy stuff. People got so drunk they'd pass out in our yard, and often they'd still be there the next morning sleeping it off. I remember thinking how strange it was when I'd see men with their arms around women that weren't their wives, and vice-versa. All kinds of debauchery.

Don't forget, these were all people from the church. It was not out of the ordinary to have fights and yelling one minute, and everyone singing loudly with a crude country song the next. I'd go to bed and wake up to people all over our house, sleeping on the floors and in the yard. It was my job to clean it all up. Beer cans and bottles everywhere and all kinds of trash, and other stuff, that I shouldn't have seen. My task was to keep my mouth shut and clean it up.

My dad started to be a little nicer to me after I turned ten years old. He'd tell me, "You act like a man, and I'll treat you like one." All I wanted was to make him proud of me, so I did my best. Sometimes he'd open a can of beer and give it to me when we sat by the campfire.

"Wow!" I thought, "this is great. If I act like a man, he wouldn't beat me up so often, and all I have to do is keep my mouth shut and drink beer with him!" I now think that he was starting to groom me to be just like him; a drunken dirt-bag.

Have you ever watched an old western? You know, the old black and white westerns where the bad guys always had black hats, and the good guys wore white ones? I know this might sound strange, but that's what I always wanted to be as a kid, "a White Hat."

I'd watch those old westerns and get so happy when the White Hat guy would get through a tough spot, beating the Black Hats at their evil plans. I know it seems weird, but it was a core thing in me. I wanted to do good and not bad. That's not saying I was good, no, no one is, but I had a different compass in me that didn't point the same way my dad's compass did. I felt like my dad was a Black Hat trying to turn me from my dream of being good.

There was a time when I thought "OK, maybe I'm as bad as they say I am, I'm going to be a Black Hat and be bad." It felt horrible. I just wasn't that guy, but how do you hide a White Hat in the Black Hat's lair? It was tough.

I poured myself into what I thought would make my dad proud of me hoping I could impress him with my skills, and he wouldn't notice that I wasn't like him. He loved to hunt and be in the outdoors. I tried to be someone who could survive in the wild with only one match and no food. I learned to shoot a gun and a bow and arrow really well. I'd catch fish and crawdads in the creek and cook them over a fire in the rain. All these things I did to try and stand out to my dad and have value or worth in his eyes.

Feeling worthless is something I've struggled with since my youth. It's a scar that has plagued me for so long. I was trying to show my dad my value and The Stepmother was trying to gut me of any value I might have ever had. The more my dad showed me attention, the more she would attack me physically and mentally.

That White Hat I wanted so desperately to wear seemed like it was turning gray, and was continually being knocked off by her flying monkeys.

12

♦

The Ship and the Whip

The Stepmother's mom, Grandma Laura-Lee, had Parkinson's disease, and we were at her house a lot of the time, taking care of her. The Stepmother's dad was always away working or whatever he did. He was a creepy man. I was glad when he wasn't there.

The Parkinson's had taken its toll on Grandma Laura-Lee. Her hands would shake without stopping; it had gotten bad enough that we had to help her eat. We also had to wipe her mouth for her because she would drool, and it was just sad to watch. She struggled to keep her eyes open, so we would push her eyelids open and turn the TV to whatever she wanted to watch. She could hardly get out of her chair without someone pulling her arms and helping her up.

I liked her, she was Grandma to me. She was nice. She had a good sense of humor and thought it funny when I once tied a sponge to her chin to soak up the drool. I thought I was being smart, finding a solution to the problem so we didn't have to wipe her chin so often. She laughed and thought it was so funny, saying I was very clever. Oops! No one else thought it was a good idea.

We liked to play games together, like I'd hide a thimble in the room, and she would look for it from her chair. Sometimes, she would count the seconds I could hold my breath and cheer when I'd break my record. All kinds of fun little games like that. She also taught me how to do math in my head that's really quick. It really helped me; I use it, even to this day. She was kind to me, and I loved her for that.

This day, when we were at Grandmas house, I was in the living room, feeling bored, flipping my slipper off my foot and trying to catch it again. I almost had it when…I flipped it too hard. I can still see it flying across the living room to the top of the bookcase. CRASH! I was horrified as I watched it smash into a glass ship that was displayed on the top shelf. This ship was made of blown glass and was The Stepmothers dad's prize possession.

The Stepmother came running into the living room like a lion on the attack. She looked at the ship and then at me. Her eyes seemed to turn red with anger. She grabbed me by the hair and dragged me into a spare bedroom at the other end of the house. She started slapping me and then punching me. It was hurting her hand, so she grabbed a plastic hairbrush and started hitting me with it until it broke in two. She then grabbed a ruler that was on the desk and broke that also. She stomped out of the room and returned with a large wooden spoon with a heavy handle, that broke after a few blows. Then she went and grabbed a large plastic ladle. That broke as well. She grabbed a few other things that were laying around, breaking all of them across my back. She then grabbed a handful of wire hangers. "YOU WON'T BREAK THESE!" she yelled.

I'm telling you being whipped with a wire hanger is a pain like no other. She went crazy whipping me from my head to my calves. It hurt so bad. The backs of my arms were on fire with pain. I saw stars as a blow landed to the back of my head. I tried to block the blows with my hands, and she hit my knuckles with a sting. They instantly turned black and swelled to twice their size as my hand quit working. I was trying to get away, but she had me by the hair whipping and cussing me in a frenzy. The pain was almost unbearable, especially when the whips hit the soft skin around the kidney area. It went on and on.

That's when Grandma Laura-Lee almost fell as she entered the room, sliding against the wall as she used it to stand. She was yelling at her daughter to "STOP!" She was doing her best to get in between us to stop the attack. How had she gotten out of her chair? How had she made it from her chair to the room we were in? It had to have taken everything she had to walk in there to save me. She was sobbing as she yelled at The Stepmother in her disgust. The Stepmother let me go as she turned to yell back at her mother.

I made my way into the bathroom to tend to my wounds. It was horrible. It hurt so bad. I took off my shirt and looked in the mirror. It looked like I'd been whipped like a slave. Large, long, bloody welts crisscrossed my back and legs. My hands were bruised, and I couldn't move a few knuckles. I was sick with the adrenaline running through my system. Grandma Laura-Lee inspected my wounds the best she could, as she cried. She had me get into a cold bath to try and stop the swelling. I was sick to my stomach. The pain was so bad I thought I was going to throw up. I thought I might pass out, too. My body shivered in shock as I crawled into the bath, the cold water stinging my wounds. I laid there in the cold water and wept. I had no words, just tears.

When I got out of the bath, The Stepmother had gone. She'd left me there as she stormed off. I didn't go home that night. Grandma had me stay the night at her house. I put cool wet towels on my back most of the night to help the fevered welts from stinging too bad. I got to have ice cream for dinner though, that was a plus. I couldn't stop shaking all night long and that weird breathing thing you do when you've been sobbing, you know, like you can't quite catch your breath.

The next day, my dad picked me up and took me home. He talked to me about how I needed to control myself and not break things. I said, "OK, I'm sorry I messed up." The Stepmother wouldn't even look at me on my return. It was like my presence disgusted her. I stayed as far away from her as I could for weeks after that.

After a few weeks had passed, The Stepmother confronted me as I was walking out of my bedroom in the garage. She scolded me on how bad I was and said that her dad was so mad at me because I'd broken his glass ship. She said that he didn't want to see me for a while. She tried to tell me it was my fault that I'd been "spanked so long," in her words, because I wouldn't stand still and just take my punishment. I just stood there not saying a word as she went on and on telling me how worthless I was and that I'd deserved everything I'd gotten.

In mid-sentence she stopped and looked up at the ceiling. I looked up and the only thing that was up there was the attic access. It was a square access hatch into the attic. It was trimmed in the same wood that was used throughout the house around the doors and windows. A stepladder had been leaned against the wall, that we used to climb into the attic. She climbed the ladder and started prying a section of the trim off. I couldn't figure out what she was doing. She took off a short piece, that was about two and a half feet long. The trim was about three inches wide, a half of an inch thick on one edge, tapering to about a quarter of an inch at the other edge.

She climbed down and stood there holding it in one hand as she lightly tapped it into her other hand, like she was checking the weight. She said, "You won't be able to break this." She bent over the nails that were poking through the wood on one side.

I looked at her new weapon that she was bouncing into her hand. I also saw the evil look come across her face too, like she'd found a new toy to torture me with. I hadn't quite healed up from the last attack and I had my back to my room. I felt trapped and was wondering what she was going to do next. She just smiled at me with an evil grin as she walked back into the house, putting the club on top of the refrigerator, with about six inches sticking out, just in case she needed to grab it quick. It didn't take her long before she got to try her new toy out on me.

The Stepmother was very crafty in her evil towards me. On this day she decided to trick me with a challenge. The challenge was, she would tie me to a chair, and she bet me that I couldn't escape. I was always into survival, as I had said before, and thought I would be able to escape, no problem. How could I have been so stupid?

She tied the ropes extremely tight. I started to try and wriggle my way out. This is when she started to taunt me. She began to pinch me. And then started to slap me. She began to slap and hit a little bit harder, trying to get a reaction out of me, while her taunting intensified. She wanted a reaction that would justify the increasing abuse. I was getting frustrated and angry. Not only at the situation, but at myself for letting her trick me. I realized that me escaping wasn't her main objective. She wanted to try out her new weapon.

She went and grabbed it from the top of the fridge and started using it on me. She was being very strategic where she hit me as I tried to bounce away from her blows until falling over on my side. I was like a turtle on its back with my hands tied to the chair. The flat side hit with a slap and hurt, leaving its mark, but when she used the thick edge, it bruised to the bone. I don't know if an x-ray can tell if bones were once broken or not, but I'd bet if it could, it would show I walked away from that attack with a couple of broken ribs.

Again, I ask, why did she hate me so bad? These attacks were way beyond a normal dislike for someone or even for someone who's considered a harsh disciplinarian. These were pure hate-fueled attacks, with an almost unstoppable rage driving them.

I'd try and tell my dad that something was wrong, but he never wanted to hear it. He'd always say, "just stop being bad and get along with her." He didn't seem to care what she was doing. I don't think they were speaking that much anymore. Something was definitely going on behind the scenes that I didn't know about at the time. My dad never stopped having his affairs, and I think she knew about them. Because of this, her hate for me grew stronger. I was doomed.

I would find out later what really had fueled her hate for me, but that will have to wait awhile.

13

Get A Job

The wild parties continued at our house; they were happening even more often now. My parents' friends slowly changed to a new crowd, the crowd that was seen most often at the parties. Because of this, my friends started to fade away from me as well, until finally, when I was almost twelve years old, they just seemed to forget about me entirely.

Our washer and dryer had quit working, and we were poor. My parents spent more on drink than food or bills. We had to go to town to wash our clothes at the laundro-mat. My dad had been working on the side for a good guy named Dan. Dan was a painter by trade and his son was one of the last friends who would still talk to me. They'd grown up poor as well and sympathized with us.

My dad had been working for Dan at night and on weekends trying to get some money saved to buy a washer and dryer. Things were going well when he let it slip to Dan that only a couple more jobs and he'd have the money to buy that new hunting rifle he'd been wanting. Dan was upset because he'd been giving my dad extra work to help us buy a washer and a dryer. They had words and my dad didn't work for him anymore.

I was asleep one night when my friend and his older brother walked into my room. "What are you doing here?" I asked.

They said, "Get up! We brought cake!"

Cake! I love cake and didn't get it very often. I went out of my room and there were two large boxes in our living room.

"What are those?"

"A washer and a dryer," they said.

Cake and a washer and dryer! That's great! I was sitting at the table eating cake with them and looking out the back glass door, that was open to the yard. My dad was out by the fire pit drinking, like he often did. Dan was out there talking to him, explaining that he didn't approve of my dad being dishonest with him about the work and that he was sorry that they'd had words. Dan had bought the washer and dryer for us because someone had done that for them as well, when they were struggling to make ends meet. Dan was a good guy and wanted to pay it forward, as it were.

My dad was drunk and falling down. I remember watching Dan trying to help my dad back towards the house in his drunken state. My dad was yelling at Dan, saying, "I don't need your *blankety blank* charity!" as he leaned against Dan, while Dan helped my dad stumble back to the house.

I was always watching everything, trying to read every situation, and every move. Looking for the danger and when to run from it. I watched as my dad yelled at Dan again. "I don't need your charity!" Just then, my dad stepped back and puked all over Dan's legs and feet. Dan just dropped him in disgust. He stood there for a second as my dad yelled something at him that I couldn't hear.

Dan didn't say a word to him, he just looked at my dad for a second then walked up to the house and grabbed the hose, washing off the vomit. He said to his wife, "Nita, grab the kids, let's go."

That was the last time I would see my friend for a very long time.

It would be almost four years until they came back into my story. And just like that, I was alone again.

All my friends were now gone. The Stepmother told me it was because I was a loser and weird. I started to believe what she told me, that something was wrong with me. I couldn't figure it out. What was wrong with me, and how could I fix it?

No one hated me more than the one looking back at me in the mirror. We were poor and I felt it made me lesser than everyone else.

Maybe if I could fix that, people would like me more. But how? I'd been buying my own clothes since I was ten years old. I'd pick berries and mow yards all summer to save up enough money to get a few clothes from the secondhand store. Always buying them a little big so I had room to grow into them as the year went on.

Don't think all the kids didn't notice I'd wear the same pants to school all week and make fun of me for it. Secondhand clothes and hand me downs, that were sometimes girls' pants, made me a target. My shoes typically had holes in them, top and bottom. I'd put cardboard in them to keep my socks from getting so wet. For some reason that I will never know, The Stepmother would write my name in ink on the toes of my shoes. This would only draw attention to them, bringing me embarrassment and shame.

The Stepmother was the one who cut my hair. She'd always cut it in an odd way to make me look funny or off. Never to the style of the day or even to the typical style most people in the church had. If people talked to me, usually it was only to be mean to me. I think when you're broken as a kid, it's like being a speckled bird, it seems people can't help but pick on you. It's an odd thing in human nature to treat broken people so poorly.

Life got very lonely after all my friends went away. I wonder if it would've been better if I'd never had any friends to start with. It would have hurt way less. My dad was drinking more and more, and The Sisters and I were still enemies and would do the fight club thing from time to time. The Stepmother was getting meaner and meaner, if you could even imagine that could happen, but it did. Life was just spiraling downward.

Then on my twelfth birthday, my dad said, "Well, now you're a man, go get a job." So, I did. There was a small country store about a mile away from where we lived. They were looking for a bottle boy to sort cans, sweep up, and stock the shelves. I applied and got the job. I'd work six days a week from 4:30pm to 12:30am, and walk home after, getting home about 1:30am.

My day began early and ended late. I'd get up at 6am and I had to really hustle to get ready for school. No time for breakfast (even if there was any to be had). I had chores to do, no time to waste. I had to get out early to feed and water the chickens and the pigs before heading to school.

I'd grab my things and walk the half of a mile to the bus stop to get to school. My stop was the first on the bus route to school and the last off the bus coming home. Typically, I'd get off the bus, run home and look for something to eat, before running back up the road to get to work on time. Needless to say, I never had time to do any homework. Most days, there was very little to eat in the refrigerator, so I started going to the shed where all the home canned stuff was stored. I liked peaches. I'd open a jar and eat a few halves, and on many days, that was my dinner.

I liked working, it gave me purpose and got me out of the house. My folks required me to give them most of my paycheck and put whatever was left over (which was very little) in the bank. I would be 16 years old in a few years and I wanted to buy a car. That was my goal. I became invisible at work, most of the time, and that was OK by me. I found my routine and it was good.

I remember the day when the store got a deli case. It had fried chicken and burritos in it. I loved fried chicken and would always hope some of the pieces wouldn't be sold by the end of the night. Some nights I'd get to have a piece to eat as I walked home in the dark. I was so thin the boss told me I looked like one of those kids from the 'help the hungry kids' commercials.

The walk home every night was unnerving. I had to really take my fears captive and focus on the road ahead. Our gravel driveway was so dark, being back in the trees, and full of potholes. As I'd said before, my shoes always had holes in them, so I had to be very careful not to step in a pothole full of water. I got through it and after a while I kind of remembered where to step to avoid all the potholes.

Life went on like that for a while.

14

◆

Little Red Bible

My dad's two brothers had drifted away from us for years due to my dad's drinking and rough lifestyle. Their parents had ended up leaving the church during that time also because my grandmother found out she needed heart surgery. They'd been sneaking to the hospital, and it was found out. It caused issues in the church and the family, so they left. After my grandparents left the church, I didn't get to see them that often anymore.

When I did get to see my uncles, I really liked them. My oldest uncle was very jolly, laughing all the time. He was a really nice guy too. I've often wondered how he was so great and his brother, my dad, was such a dirt-bag.

The oldest uncle had a dairy farm, and we'd go over there once in a while when I was younger, before there was trouble between the brothers. I liked going to the dairy and seeing all the cows and fancy birds they had in a big pen. My older cousin probably thought I was a nuisance following him around asking questions, and when I'd just sit there watching him play his guitar on the porch by his room. I may have bugged him, but he was never mean to me. I thought he was the coolest guy I'd ever met. You know what? He still is.

My uncle got sick one spring after he'd sprayed his fruit trees with some kind of poison. He was sick for months. My dad and his younger brother had to milk the cows for him and take care of the farm. On my days off from work I'd help milk the cows too. After many months, the decision was made to sell the dairy and move to town. I think this broke my uncle's heart, but he adjusted after a time. We helped them move and one of my jobs was to burn the big piles of trash and old boxes and things. I had a big fire going, slowly throwing boxes in, one at a time.

I had just thrown a box on the fire when it tumbled back towards me, the contents spilling out into the fire. When this happened, I noticed a small red book had tumbled out. I don't know how, but I knew right away that it was a small Bible. I took a stick and quickly fished the book out of the fire before it was burned. I grabbed it, and yes, it was a Bible. I'd never looked in a Bible before. I knew it was where God lived, and to me, it was like a book of magic, something to be cherished.

Why was my uncle throwing a Bible away? It must have been a mistake. I thought it was a really bad thing to burn a Bible. I looked the Bible over for damage, like a little red treasure in my hands. I wanted to keep that book so bad, but wait… what if it was a bad Bible? I'd heard there were Bibles that were "bad" or different than the ones the church read. Maybe this was one of those Bibles? I looked it over and, on the front, it said New Testament. There was a small diamond shape, then Psalms & Proverbs, and a shape that looked like a two handled jug inside of a circle, near the bottom of the cover. I just didn't know if it was a good or a bad Bible. What do I do? I wanted to keep it so bad.

My uncle always kept a Bible on the back of the toilet. "That Bible must be a good Bible if it was in his house," I thought. "I know what I'll do… I'll go into the bathroom and compare the books."

I went in and locked the door. I didn't want anyone to know I had it. I feared it would be taken away from me. I began comparing the two Bibles. I opened each and saw the name "King James." I wondered who he was? OK, that matched up in both books. I looked further. Matthew, Mark, Luke, and John. Hmm, that was the same too. It all seemed to match up. Oh, how I wanted to keep that little red book. So, I decided to put it in my pocket and hide it from everyone when I got home. I felt really guilty, but I wanted to keep it and tried to convince myself that it was like finding something in the trash. Finders' keepers.

I got it home and looked it over. I wondered who all these people in the Bible were? Who was Matthew? I'll start reading there.

I would try and read it after I'd get home from work at 1:30 in the morning before I'd fall asleep. I was so confused at what a "Begot" was. I went to the library at school and looked the word up. Oh, it's like generations of people that were related, OK, I got it now.

The little bit I read didn't make sense to me. I'd fall asleep most of the time just a page or two in, only to restart at the beginning the next night. I felt I had to hide the Bible from my parents because I thought they would take it from me. I knew God was in that book somewhere and I was so curious to try and find Him. But after a while of trying to read it, I gave up. It was so confusing. I kept the Bible just in case I needed it. I still have that little red Bible; it turns out it's a Gideons Pocket Bible.

Years later, I confessed to my uncle that I'd taken the Bible from the fire and kept it and that I'd felt guilty about it since that day. He laughed and said that it was OK, I could keep it with no guilt or worries attached.

Life went on with more and more pressure from my dad to be his drinking buddy and not his son. Sadly, I tried to find my path in his world for a time. I wanted his approval and was also so tired of being alone. When we'd go hunting or camping, my dad would ask me what kind of whiskey I wanted for the trip. He'd buy me a couple of bottles of whatever I asked for, and it just seemed normal. We'd also pack several cases of beer too. He'd get all liquored up and start talking about women in ways that made me blush and uncomfortable. His plan seemed to be, he'd get me hooked on booze, and then when I was old enough, the women too. We'd be a dirt-bag duo.

I felt like I was trapped in quicksand, being slowly pulled under. My desire to find God in the little red Bible seemed to be at odds with the lifestyle I was being drawn into. It went on like that for a couple of years, a tug of war for my attention between the darkness and the light. I thought I was acting like a man, just like my dad had told me too, but in reality, the darkness wasn't that much fun, and I came to realize that I didn't want the future my dad had planned for me.

I felt lost, and didn't know what to do.

15

Jail Bird

I was working all the time and didn't have much to show for it. I was fifteen now and under a lot of pressure. The Stepmother, all of a sudden, decided I needed to fit into the Follower kids' group. "Just jump into one of the teenagers' cars after church and go with them," she'd say. What? That's not how it's done. You don't just jump into someone's car. It was so humiliating having to ask these total strangers if I could go with them. Only once or twice did I ever get a ride. The Stepmother would get so mad at me when I'd get back into our car after church, failing to get a ride with one of the guys.

One Sunday, she dropped me off at the movie theater that I'd heard all the guys were going to after church. Again, she told me, "Just jump in after the movie and get a ride with them." I knew this was a really bad idea. After the movie was over, they got in their cars and drove away leaving me there on the steps. I just stood there watching as they all left. I sat outside on the steps for a long time before I called home to get picked up. I watched a train go by and thought about jumping on it and hoping it would take me far, far away. But I didn't.

When The Stepmother got there, true to form, I was shamed all the way home. Every once in a while, on the hour-long drive, she'd stop the car and spin around, to slap me and tell me how worthless I was. I wanted to find a hole and climb into it.

The church had a dance every Sunday night for all the teenagers so we had something to do, and to keep the Follower kids away from the world. I'd had to help the Older Sister learn how to dance a few years before and I wasn't too bad at it, but The Stepmother forced me to go out to the party and dance with the kids. I knew no one. It was really scary.

The boys that I had been forced to ask for a ride with were extra mean to me. The girls were all so pretty and I had no idea what to say to them. At a dance party at the church, when the music would start the boys would go over and pick a girl to dance, by tapping her on the shoulder. Some girls would walk away from me, and others would say "No." This was going to be much harder than I thought.

Finally, one said "Yes," and we danced, and then a few more said "Yes." The way the Followers dance is like a country two-step style of dancing. Two steps forward and one step back to the rhythm.

I would introduce myself and tell them my name and ask who they were. My wife was one of those girls that I would dance with, asking her name. She has since told me how it was very odd that I didn't know anyone, and even more so, that I thought no one knew who I was. What I didn't understand is that the children at Followers are put together at a young age, and everyone knows everyone else. At the time, I didn't realize how isolated I really was.

It was like I had been dropped in from outer space. I liked talking to the girls and dancing was fun, so it was worth it, even when the older boys were mean to me.

Most of the kids treated me with a distant curiosity. I always felt watched or judged. This went on for about a year. I worked every other Sunday, and I'd need a ride to and from the parties on the

Sundays that I didn't work. I couldn't drive yet. Usually, to get to a party you came with the friends you were with that day, but I didn't have the luxury of friends. And the Older Sister couldn't take me home because she went on dates or carloads after the parties. That said, I didn't get to go to the parties very often.

I finally turned sixteen years old and got my driver's license. I'd saved about $600 in the bank over the last four years and wanted to buy a car. There was a problem though—my bank account was empty. Where was my money?

My dad told me they needed it for bills. I was so mad at him. He had an old Datsun pickup that didn't run very well. I told him, "I want your truck in trade!" The Stepmother was mad that I'd even suggest it, but my dad looked guilty that he'd taken my money and agreed to give me the keys, but only under one condition: I had to buy *them* a car.

The Stepmother's dad was selling an old piece of junk for $500, and I could buy it on credit. I agreed and I had my first car and freedom (ish). My dad instantly grounded me for two weeks for my arrogance and "to show me that he still could." Well, I got to wash my car in the yard for two weeks and dream of the open road and freedom.

After the grounding was over, I quit the store and got a job at Chick-Fil-A. It was 1986 and there were two Chick-Fil-A's in my area that were owned by the same man. After he died the franchise was lost and not to return to the area until many years later. I really liked working there. It paid a lot more than the store, and Chick-Fil-A is closed on Sundays. I could go to the parties on Sunday nights and dance with those girls. Yahoo! I didn't know then, but my life was soon to change in a way I never would have imagined.

By now, it was January 1987, and I'd had a few months of driving and freedom. Sadly, the little truck I'd made the trade for had a bad engine and stopped working only four months after getting it. I was now the taxi for everyone, driving the junk car I'd had to buy for the family. I was made to take my Little Sister here and there and then go get her. If my dad was up at the tavern drunk and needed a ride home, it was me they sent. I also used the car to go to work.

On one Thursday night, my dad was in the middle of one of his rants about if I ever get arrested, he's going to leave me there to rot. I remember thinking, "Yeah, yeah... I never do anything but work and drive everyone around."

The next night was Friday and there was a wedding out at the church. A few of my old friends had started to speak to me again, I think it was probably because I could drive. My friends were planning on going to get a hamburger after the wedding. I thought "Yes! They want to hang out with me!" and begged my folks to use the car. They said no to the car, but I could go with them if someone else drove a different car. The boys and I found a ride with one guy that I'd never spoken to before. He was looking for a different group of friends to start hanging out with.

Well...after getting the hamburger, we ended up driving around and noticed there was a ladder leaning up against the wall at the back of the shopping center in town. "Hey!" we thought, "let's climb up and take a look around!"

As we looked around, to my horror, I saw a couple of police cars driving in. They had seen us up there and we were in trouble.

I guess there had been several break-ins at the shopping center recently, through the roof. And the cops thought maybe we were the perpetrators. They yelled at us to "GET ON YOUR FACES!" with their guns drawn, and then we were put into police cars and taken to the local jail.

Ugh! Really? Did it have to be the very next day after my dad had warned me to not get arrested!?

Yep, I got arrested. Yep, he was not happy when the cops called him to come pick me up. When the cops called my dad, they said "Sir, your son has been arrested, and you need to come pick him up."

My dad said "Nope, keep him!" And he hung up the phone.

They continued to call him back until 3AM. I begged them to please stop. I said to them, "I'll stay here in jail!"

They told me "No," and called him again. This time they threatened him, then told him he had to come and get me. "Oh great!" I thought, "now you've really made him mad." When he finally showed up, he was red with anger.

All the other kids' dads had been there hours before to get their sons. My dad was really upset to be there. A very large officer got right in my dad's face and told him if he even said one word to me before we got home, he was going to throw my dad in jail.

"Please stop!" I thought. "Please!"

My dad agreed and the cop walked us to the car, walking between my dad and me. He then put me in the backseat directly behind him. The cop told my dad we were just being boys and didn't do anything that bad. My dad said nothing. The cop followed us home for a while. It was pure silence. After we got home...not so much.

It went as you could imagine. He yelled and smacked me around, told me how disappointed he was. He told me that I was going to wish that he had left me in that jail. He told me he was going to make sure I wasn't around those boys ever again, even went so far as to call the other dads trying to strong arm them into not allowing us to be around each other anymore. Then he grounded me for a month. I was grounded from everything. No church, no parties, no anything but school and work, and I had to give him most of my pay.

When I wasn't at work or school, they had all kinds of crazy chores for me to do. I guess I had it coming a little. He had warned me not to get arrested. And he was true to his word. I did wish I could have stayed in the jail for the month, I would have had a better time.

I finally got past the long 30 days and went back to normal life. Several kids talked to me about what had happened. The strict punishment seemed to really make an impression on people. I thought "Wow! How very odd…"

Most of these people had never even talked to me before, and now all of the sudden people seemed to care.

16

The Last Battle

My first nephew was born February 18, 1987. My older sister had gotten married a couple years before and had been staying at our house for ten days after the birth. The women at the church don't go to the hospital to have babies, they have them at home with a church midwife. This is considered a lay midwife, and the only training these women have is attending other births. In the tradition of the church, most first babies are born at your parents' house. The new mothers then stay in bed for ten days to heal after the birth and women from the church bring dinner every night for ten days. I thought it was great having so much food and desserts around.

It was now March 1987. My older sister and her husband had gone home that day from her "ten days", and my little sister and I were returning from a Sunday night party. It was about 9:30 in the evening, when we walked into the house, and my dad true to form was passed out in his chair surrounded by beer cans. He'd had to be on his best behavior for the past ten days, and I guess he took the first opportunity to get smashed.

My little sister and I didn't get along, as I'm sure you may have gathered from the story you've been reading. When I entered the kitchen, I saw a large piece of pie in a glass dish on the kitchen counter. I grabbed it. The piece of pie was large enough to share, but

I was being a jerk and not giving any to my sister. I'd learned to be very quiet in everything I did, never bringing attention to myself when I was at home. This made me less of a chance to be a target. My little sister hadn't had to worry as much as I did because she was always protected by The Stepmother. Sometimes my dad would get angry and rough her up, but not that often.

My little sister had a mouth on her, and she was very loud too. She liked to yell, thinking if she was loud, she would get what she wanted. Typically, this worked well for her. My dad didn't like it though, and when she started acting like her "big mouth mother," (in his words) he would smack her across the face.

Well, as you can imagine, she wasn't happy that I was not sharing the pie with her. She started yelling at me as I sat at the table, trying my best to ignore her. All of the sudden, my dad jumped up out of his chair and came into the kitchen, grabbing my little sister by the shirt. I watched as he slapped her across the face, once, then again and again. She was screaming for her mother, but she never came to save her this time. I think The Stepmother was passed out in her room.

I looked up and my dad's hand had turned into a fist as he was smacking my sister around. I sat there looking down at the pie for a second and something in me snapped. I stood up and yelled at him to stop hitting her. I yelled, "If you want someone to hit, hit me! It was my fault!"

My dad stopped and just looked at me with a surprised look on his face. I was only sixteen years old and maybe 100 pounds. I thought to myself, "WHAT AM I DOING?!" I stood there with my fists up ready to fight—I'd had it!

He just stood there looking at me in a daze. This gave my little sister a chance to escape to her room to hide. My dad just wiped his face and said nothing to me, as he staggered down the hallway to his room. I quickly went to my room and thought, "Oh he's not going to let this pass. He'll be back to get me any minute." I waited with my shoes on. I was ready, but unfortunately, I fell asleep after waiting for about an hour or more.

The next thing I remember is being pulled out of my bed by my hair as my dad was kicking me in the stomach. I landed on my face on the floor. He still had me by the hair and was cussing me out, screaming, "YOU THINK YOU'RE TOUGH, YOU LITTLE #$*!" The Stepmother was standing in the doorway blocking any escape, cheering him on in his attack.

He kicked the wind out of me and then kicked me once in the face. I was bleeding now and trying to get free from his grasp on my hair. I finally twisted free and as I got to my feet, I was met with a punch to the mouth. This knocked me back towards my bed. I started to try and move towards the door to escape, but The Stepmother took a swing at me from the doorway, just missing me as I dodged the blow.

Remember, my room was more of a large closet than an actual bedroom in size. It was close quarters fighting with very little room for three people to move around. I was trapped and had to fight. I dodged a blow from The Stepmother as my dad jumped on me. Like I said, I was about 100 pounds, and he was probably closer to 250. His weight was crushing me against my bed as he lay on me, punching me in the face. He had me in a headlock as he continued to punch me. I reached my right arm around his head trying to dig out his eye with my thumb. He tried to bite my hand in his defense. His teeth almost had me when I stuck my pointer finger in his mouth pulling as hard as I could at the corner of his lip, trying to rip his mouth open to his cheek.

This hurt him and he was cussing up a storm. I pulled as hard as I could, hoping to rip his face off. He was trying to bite off my finger but couldn't shake my grip. He finally let go of my head to grab at my hand in his mouth. I squirmed out from under him and stood to face off again.

The Stepmother took another swing at me from the doorway when my dad ran at me again. I was able to lean back quickly against my bed and get my feet up against him, kicking back at him as he attacked. He'd come at me with a punch, and I'd kick him with everything I had. I didn't care where it landed. We did that a few times when he grabbed my foot and dragged me off the bed to the floor.

The floor is not a good place to be in a fight. I kicked and kicked at him as he kicked back at me. I got to my feet, and he took a few punches at me until he stopped, too winded to move.

The Stepmother was cussing me and saying, "YOU THINK YOU'RE TOUGH?! FIGHT LIKE A MAN AND STOP KICKING LIKE A COWARD!"

I yelled, "IF YOU WANT TO FIGHT, LET'S GO OUTSIDE AND DO IT!"

My dad yelled, "FINE, LET'S GO!" and we went into the back yard.

I had only one shoe on with no sock and my shirt was torn in half. I was bleeding from my mouth and my nose, and my eye was starting to swell shut. I wiped the blood away with what was left of my shirt, before squaring off with my dad. He took a swing at me—I ducked it. I took a swing back, hitting him in the stomach. He grabbed me, throwing me to the ground, trying to kick me again. I rolled away from him, jumping to my feet as he landed a few blows. He was drunk and fat and out of breath. His blows weren't as fast as they had been, and he was breathing really heavy.

The Stepmother was yelling at me, "OH! YOU ARE SO @$%&& GONE! YOU'RE NOT LIVING HERE ANYMORE! YOU PIECE OF @#@%!" My dad was leaning against the house, pointing at me in disgust, breathing too heavy to talk.

I thought, "That's it, I'm done! I'm not staying here anymore!" I went back into the garage and headed to my room to get a shoe and a shirt back on. As I entered my room, I heard footsteps running at me from behind. I spun around as my dad landed another blow. The fight was back on and back in my room. Back against the bed in more of a wrestling match than a fist fight.

He punched me in the face, and I hit him in the ear. I kneed him in the leg as he tried to lay on me to crush me with his weight. I was able to get my foot up and kick him in the stomach again. This forced him back a few steps, that's when I launched my attack! I jumped up and swung as fast as I could and as many times as I could, hitting him in the face. I watched as his nose fell to the side, blood squirting out across his face. His eyes were wide with surprise that I'd landed so many blows. I was on fire with rage and not feeling anything anymore, just anger.

I yelled, "COME ON!" as I stood there with my fists up ready for another attack.

The wind was knocked out of his attack as he grabbed his bleeding face. He walked out of my room past The Stepmother. She yelled at him, calling him a quitter, then turned on me. I turned towards her with my fists up ready to break her nose too, if she came at me. She just spit on me as she turned and walked away. I grabbed a shoe and a tee-shirt, putting them on. I also grabbed one other tee-shirt and put it in a plastic bag that was lying on the floor.

I headed out the side door and was about to head out through the woods towards the direction of town. My little sister had climbed out of her window and ran towards me, begging me not to go. "I can't stay here anymore," I said.

She begged, "Please stay! Who will protect me from them if you leave?"

I was still burning hot with anger as I looked from the shadows where we were standing. Looking back towards the house. I could see my dad sitting at the table in the kitchen holding a towel to his face, trying to stop his nose from bleeding. I could see The Stepmother standing there yelling at him. I said to my little sister, "You stay hidden in the woods and don't come out until I come and get you."

Out in the garage my dad kept a few guns in a case. I knew where they were, and I knew how to use them. I snuck back into the garage going to the case, finding a 22-caliber pistol. I loaded it and then stormed in through the garage door, into the house to confront him. My dad's eyes were wide as I stood there with a gun in my hand. He knew I knew how to shoot because he'd taught me.

The Stepmother stood a few feet behind him with her eyes and mouth wide open, not saying a word for the first time ever. My dad wasn't moving as he held the towel to his face covering his nose and mouth.

I screamed at him, "IF YOU EVER TOUCH MY LITTLE SISTER AGAIN, I'LL KILL YOU!"

He just sat there looking at me, then at the gun in my hand. A part of me wanted him to make a try for the gun, giving me reason to shoot him between the eyes. I yelled at him again as I was filled with rage.

"DID YOU HEAR ME? IF YOU TOUCH HER AGAIN, I'LL KILL YOU!"

With his eyes wide, he slowly nodded, saying nothing. I backed out the door into the garage, slamming the door as hard as I could, hearing the dishes crash in the hutch that was near the door. I ran outside to my sister. She was crying and begging me to stay. I couldn't…and I had to go fast and hide before my dad came after me with his gun. I knew he wouldn't sit there long before he came after me. I ran away into the woods and hid for a while. He wouldn't follow me into the woods. He knew he'd never catch me out there in the dark.

From my house to town was about seven miles by the road. If I cut through the vast woods, I could cut a few miles off. I had no plan on where I would go. I had a gun and a tee-shirt and no money… no anything really. I walked and walked, jumping into the brush if I saw headlights coming down the road. I just knew my dad was out hunting me, and it would be a gun fight if he found me.

I made it to town without him finding me. During the long walk, I remembered what one of my old friends' mom had said. Her name was Wanita, she was the wife of Dan, the same Dan who had bought us the washer and dryer. She had told me once, "I know your life is crap, if you ever need a place to stay, you come talk to me."

I thought "OK, I'll head over to their house and see if I can stay the night and figure out a plan tomorrow."

It was about 1:30 in the morning when I got there, and everything was dark. I stood outside of their door for a long time before I had the courage to knock. I knocked and a light turned on, then Dan answered the door. He thought I'd been in a car wreck because my face was all swollen and covered in dried blood. Handfuls of loose hair hung from my head from it being ripped out. Needless to say, I was a mess.

They invited me in and got me a wet towel for my face. I told them, "My dad and I had a fight. I can't go back. Can I stay the night? I'll be gone tomorrow after I figure out what to do." They said yes, and that I didn't have to leave tomorrow. They would help me figure out what to do next.

I told them about the fight and my fears for my sister. They said it was late, and we could talk tomorrow. They let me sleep in and I didn't go to school the next day. Wanita met me with breakfast and orange juice. Wow! What a treat! I almost never got orange juice!

My friend was there too. The word had gotten out to the church that I was at their house, and what had happened with my dad. The phone started ringing off the hook from people wanting to talk to me. Some wanted to give me encouragement and others wanted to make sure I wouldn't tell on them for going to my dad's wild parties. I said I wouldn't tell on them as long as they left me alone. A cousin of my dad's came over with clothes for me that she had just bought: pants, a shirt, and a jean coat. All this attention was very odd to me and made me nervous. Dan and Wanita offered to let me stay another night with them, and I agreed. I didn't have anywhere else to go and was thinking maybe I could get an apartment, but I was only sixteen and had no money.

Dan and I were sitting in the living room of their house when the front door flew open, and my dad walked in. He hadn't knocked on the door, he just walked in like he owned the place. It had been a couple of days since I'd left home, and he'd heard where I was staying. My heart stopped. I thought he was there to kill me, as I looked in his hands for his gun. He just yelled at me to get my stuff and get in the car. I didn't want trouble at Dan's house. They'd been so good to me. I knew this was going to go badly with my dad and me. One of us would probably die if I went back.

I jumped up and went to the room that they had let me stay in, out back off of their family room. I grabbed my gun and stuck it in the back of my pants, making sure it was loaded and ready to use. I was headed back in from the family room when Wanita stopped me by standing in the doorway.

She said, "Where do you think you're going?"

I said, "I have to go," as I tried to push past her.

She said, "No, you don't," as she wrapped her arms around me, holding me in place.

I said to her, "It can't happen here." I didn't really want to leave, but I also thought my dad might start shooting in their house and I didn't want that.

Remember, my world was very, very different than most people's. My dad was a very vengeful person and I'd seen him shoot a guy's boat when we were on a lake. They were fishing next to us, and he shot their boat because they shot my fish as I reeled it in. He always

104

had his gun close by and wasn't afraid to point it at whoever was upsetting him. Most people would never fear that their dad would shoot them out of spite. But most dads wouldn't kick their kids in the face either or beat them until they pee blood.

Sadly, my dad wasn't like most dads.

Wanita had grabbed me, stopping me from going out to my dad. Truthfully, I wasn't fighting too hard to get free from her embrace. I didn't want to go. That's when I heard Dan yelling at my dad in his booming voice.

Dan always reminded me of John Wayne. He was a big man, tall and strong, with a loud deep voice. My dad wasn't. I heard Dan say to my dad, "So you think you're a tough guy beating up on a kid?" Dan was yelling now, and I could tell by the interaction that he was in my dad's face. They yelled at each other for a few minutes until Dan threw my dad out of the house threatening him if he ever came back, he would knock him out. I heard the front door slam, and the deadbolt go click.

No one other than my Grandma Laura-Lee had ever stood up for me, but Dan just had.

Dan yelled my name to come into the living room. I did and started apologizing to him for the trouble in his house. I just knew he was going to tell me that it was time for me to leave.

Dan said, "Sit down and stop talking. Do you like it here?"

"Yes," I said.

"Do you want to stay with us?" he asked.

"Yes," I said.

Dan said to me, "As long as you stay in school and stay out of trouble, you can stay here as long as you want."

I said, "I can pay you when I get some money"

He said, "Nope, you don't owe us any money, just stay out of trouble."

I said, "OK," and, "Thank you."

He said, "Go put that gun away, your dad's gone, and won't be coming back."

You can't even imagine how big of a burden that was lifted off me that day. It felt like the world's weight had just been lifted from me.

I went into the bathroom and wept.

17

◆

A New Beginning

A few days after Dan threw my dad out of their house, Wanita asked if there was anything she could do for me that would cheer me up. I said I wanted to get my hair cut by a real barber. She laughed and said that would be no problem. They let me use their car and gave me some money too. Their son, my friend Mike, and I went and got it done. I felt like a new person with only that small change. New clothes and a new haircut. It felt amazing!

My future wife noticed me that night at a church function and talked to me too. Wow! She was, and still is, so beautiful. I'd had a crush on her from the first time I'd seen her at a dance, but thought I would never have a chance with a girl like her. I was on cloud nine that she was now talking to me. I'm sure I was blushing and tongue tied as I tried to not stare at her, mesmerized by her beauty.

The next day my older sister called me at Dan's house and told me off for not going home. She was very angry, saying now everyone will know what was going on out at our house, and it will make her look bad to the church! I tried to tell her, from what I'm hearing, everyone already knew about the wild parties and crazy life we were living. She cussed at me, calling me a liar. Who did I think I was... fighting with dad!

It was very strange to me that she would be questioning me about the crazy we lived in out there, because she'd lived it too. Her anger peaked and she said that she and her husband were on their way over to Dan's house to teach me a lesson.

"ARE YOU KIDDING ME?" I demanded. "Really? You're coming over to beat me up for defending our little sister and myself?"

She just hung up the phone. I told Wanita what was going on. She called her oldest son to come over because Dan was at work. Wanita also called my dad's younger brother to see if he could come over too, just in case my older sister did make good on her threat. It was like the crazy had followed me from my old life to the new one. I didn't want it to, but there it was. I was back in the storm.

Dan and Wanita's oldest son came over in a few minutes, he is about four years older than I am. As we were talking in the living room, I looked out the window and saw my older sister and her husband drive into the driveway. Ugh! What's going to happen now? They came over to "teach me a lesson," a.k.a. beat me up. My sister was a new mother, and I wasn't going to hit her. Her husband thought he was a tough guy, cussing at me as I walked out to meet them. Dan's oldest son walked with me. My sister instantly got in his face yelling at him to mind his own business.

My brother-in-law was taking off his coat getting ready to fight me. Just then, my uncle pulled into the driveway, jumping out of his truck before it even stopped, yelling at my brother-in-law. They started pushing each other around, yelling and cussing at each other. I was just standing there shaking my head, as I watched the crazy storm rage around me. After a few minutes, my brother-in-law backed down to my uncle, telling my sister to get in the truck. They left. My uncle got back in his truck and drove off too, without saying a word to me. Then their older son did the same. I was left standing there alone in the driveway feeling sick at what had just happened. After that day, my older sister didn't speak to me again for over eight years.

Things began to drastically change for me after I ran away. All of a sudden, most people were nicer to me and would actually speak to me. I went from being invisible to being in the limelight. It was very odd.

I had so much baggage living in a peaceful home. Every time I'd flinch when Wanita would move near me, she'd grab me and hug me saying, "We'll eventually break you of that, you don't have to fear me, I'll never hit you."

I didn't know how to understand the affection either. A hug to me meant someone was too close, and I had to have my guard up, just in case of an attack. There were so many things I had to re-learn about how a normal family communicated and interacted. I was always on pins and needles thinking they would kick me out at the smallest mistake. Baggage...I had lots of baggage.

It wasn't long before my dad just disappeared. As a parting shot at me, he called the police and told them I was a drugged out runaway and dangerous. He also called the insurance company and told them the same. When I went to get insurance for a car that I bought a couple months later, it was almost impossible to find an insurance company that would take me. I finally found one, but it cost me a fortune to get basic insurance.

Soon after, I was pulled over for driving a little too fast and I was treated like a criminal by the cops. They had me get out of the car and stand on the sidewalk while they questioned me. It was kind of scary. I hadn't done anything that wrong, and they were very aggressive with me, but they didn't give me a ticket. At the time, I had no idea that my dad had called them. After answering a few questions, I thought, "How do they know all this stuff?" I asked them and they said my dad had filed a complaint against me. I told them my side of the story and they backed off a little. My dad had a DUI on his record and his character was now in question in their eyes. They said they would fill out a report that it was a false claim against me, and I shouldn't have to deal with being questioned again.

That's the kind of person my dad was.

18

A Dark Confession

After that night when I left home, my little sister and I grew closer. Maybe it was the distance or that we were both growing up... I don't know, but it was a good thing. We were happy to see each other when we had the chance.

My dad had disappeared. The Stepmother had a job somewhere, but I don't think she made much money, and my dad wasn't sending any money to help out with the bills. She was still a heavy drinker, and my little sister's clothes were looking old. School was coming soon, and I knew she needed some new school clothes, but they didn't have the money.

I sold some of my things and worked a little extra to get a couple of hundred dollars to give to her. I went to the house where they were staying now. One of The Stepmother's cousins was letting them stay in their rental for cheap. After my dad and her got a divorce, they had nowhere to live. My little sister was very happy to see me that night and very happy with the gift.

The Stepmother was drunk and her typical charming self. As I was about to leave, The Stepmother started in on me with her rebuke. She was sitting there in her chair, probably because she couldn't stand in her drunken state. She said a few venomous statements about me and that she didn't appreciate me coming over and giving my little sister money.

"We don't need your help!" she said.

I said, "I didn't do it for you." I then asked her, "Why have you always been so mean to me? What did I ever do to you?"

She said, "I've always hated you! And I've tried to make your life a living hell!"

It was almost like a venomous hiss coming from her mouth as she spoke those words.

I asked, "WHY? I was just a little kid!"

She said, "Because your dad loved you more than me!"

"Why would you say that?" I asked.

"Because it's true," she said.

Then she said something I don't think she meant to ever share with anyone. She told me, "I had every right to treat you the way I did, because..."

She was looking off into the distance as she spoke slowly to me, her gaze looking somewhere distant in her mind. I wonder if it was the drink that had torn a hole in the wall she had built around that memory.

She said her father had molested her from an early age and hadn't stopped until she'd gotten married.

Then what she said next, I think, was the thing that had broken her and what fueled her hate.

She said, "When he started molesting me, I hated it, but after a while... I got to where I enjoyed what he was doing to me."

I stood there in silence, not knowing what to say.

I could see a glimpse of how deeply she was broken and now... now I knew why. As she sat there, it was like she was holding a memory out in front of her, like a child that had taken something that wasn't hers. Then it was like she snapped out of it, pulling the memory that was in her hands back to her chest, cradling it like a baby, soaking the memory back in like a cancer, back to where she had kept it, letting it turn her heart black with hate.

She looked at me with disgust. She said, "You deserved everything I did to you because of what he did to me!"

Her hate had found its place again, and I was, and had always been, the target for its darts.

I said, "NO! I didn't deserve any of it! I wasn't the one who did those things to you. I was just a child! Why were we still around him all those years if he'd done those things to you?"

She just looked at me with hate in her eyes. She screamed "GET OUT! And don't come back!"

I turned and walked out, confused at her answers.

I guess hate needs a place to live. A place where it can grow in darkness and spread like a disease to others. Her need to punish me for the guilt that she had within her was an odd thing. Her mind had been broken by the horror, and the pleasure, not being able to reconcile the two. Not seeing it wasn't her or me that had done that to her. It was her dad and his evil disgusting actions that was the cause.

She was totally broken, mentally and emotionally. Sadly, the bottom of a bottle is where she tried to find an escape from it all. Her brokenness wasn't an excuse for treating me with such hatred. It wasn't an excuse for the beatings that almost killed me. It wasn't an excuse for the mental abuse she subjected me to everyday, leaving scars that still plague me to this day.

It wasn't an excuse for any of it.

I can understand now where that burning fire of hate came from, seeing it in her eyes when she was attacking me. Sadly, child abuse tends to link generation to generation with a chain of abuse that is so hard to break. It's because it is a learned trait, a horrible programming that a child learns and doesn't know what a normal response is when they are an adult.

I've been subject to that chain as well. I didn't know what being a good, loving dad looked like. I was way too hard on my sons. Never to the extent that I was raised with, but I was too aggressive, and I yelled when I shouldn't have, thinking if you tried harder, you could control your actions and fears.

I'm so sorry. I hope that my wife and sons will forgive me for those years I wasn't the father I should have been.

The Stepmother died years later. The drink finally took its toll. I didn't go to her funeral, I just couldn't. She had been my enemy my entire life. Literally, the monster in the dark. It surprised me that I struggled the day they put her in the ground. I didn't know how to feel. It felt wrong somehow to rejoice that she was gone. The monster that haunted my life and left me with physical and emotional scars, could only now haunt my dreams, never again to hurt me.

What were these feelings causing me to struggle? I think it was pity I felt for her, and it felt strange. Pity she was so broken, that she felt justified in doing the things she did to me. Pity that she had been abused by her dad and pity she never knew peace, drinking herself to death trying to run from the memories that haunted her.

19

♦

I Found Her

Life was so different now. I still struggled with baggage from my past, but for the most part, I just tried to fit in. Girls would talk to me now and I had friends. I went back to school and even the teachers noticed a change in me. My history teacher told me he thought I was a new student until he talked to me, welcoming me to the class. It was like the doors of the world and the church had opened to me. I was so shocked when people would call me by name, people I had no idea who they were.

After a couple of years, I convinced my future wife to be my girlfriend. I've said in this story how you will see God working, helping me through both good and really hard times. Next to grace, God's gift of my wife has been the most wonderful gift to me of all. I couldn't have made it without her.

I'd graduated from high school and was going on with life. Then one day, one of my dad's cousins gave me a photo. It was a picture of my mom and her husband. The picture also had my mom's new last name on the back of it. I told her thanks and asked how she'd gotten the photo from Texas?

"Your mom doesn't live in Texas," she told me. She said that she never had, that she'd always lived about an hour north of where I lived my entire life.

"WHAT?"

"Yep, only an hour away in the next state north of us," she said. "You should go and find her; I bet she'd love to see you."

I was so conflicted about what to do. My mom wasn't in Texas? Why hadn't she ever tried to find me all these years? Will she reject me if I find her? My heart was broken knowing she'd been so close for all those years.

One day, I decided to just go and look. It was burning me up inside and I needed to know. I drove north and went to the state police, telling them who I was, and showing them the picture of my mom. The police captain was very nice to me, and understood I wasn't a bad guy looking to hurt her, but he said he legally couldn't give me the information I was looking for.

I thought my quest was over, when he said to me, "But, if she owns property, that's public record." He told me where the public records building was, and shaking my hand, he wished me good luck.

I found the building and was directed to the basement. There were five older ladies working that day in the office. I told them my quest and they were almost all in tears rallying together to help me find my mom. After some time searching through records...

"I FOUND HER!" one of the ladies yelled excitedly, waving the paper above her head.

She wrote down the address and handed it to me. I looked at it and said, "I don't know where this is." In a whirl of activity, they found the address on a map and handed it to me, because smart phones with GPS hadn't been invented yet.

All the ladies waved to me with tears in their eyes as I thanked them and headed out. When I began to have second thoughts, they gave me encouragement that I should go and find her. They even helped me to write a letter to drop at her door, if I chickened out at the last minute.

In the letter, I explained to my mom that I felt like a piece of my life was out of place, like a puzzle piece that just wouldn't fit. I also told her about not living at home and the address of Dan and Wanita's house. I told her I knew it was dangerous for me to be reaching out to her because of the church rules and also, I was afraid Dan might kick me out if he found out that I had reached out to her. I was afraid Wanita might open the letter and read it if my mom sent me one back. I'd love to hear from her, but it came with a risk to my new life.

I waved goodbye to the ladies who had helped me and headed out. I found my mom's house and sat in the car for a long while. I ended up chickening out and just dropped the letter at her door, ringing the bell and leaving as fast as I could, full of fear of the "What ifs."

A week or two later I got a letter in the mail. It was all taped up so I could tell if someone had opened it. My mom was very happy to hear from me. She apologized that she had stayed away for so long. She said that she did it to protect us from being punished. She also acknowledged the church rules, and knew having contact with her was dangerous. She didn't want me to have any troubles, especially because of her. She asked if she could see me.

She was a nurse at a hospital only about 20 minutes' drive from where I worked. She gave me a phone number to call her to set a date and time, if I was interested in meeting with her. I talked to my girlfriend about whether I should go and see my mom. She thought it was a good idea but also knew of the danger if people found out. I called the number, and my mom answered.

It was so good to hear her voice. I was so nervous. We set a date and time right after work a few days later. I had a clean shirt in my car and combed my hair. I showed up at her work and there she was waiting for me near the door. We both had changed in the twelve years since we'd seen one another. I almost didn't recognize her, and she thought the same of me. We hugged with tears in our eyes. She seemed nervous and said she couldn't talk a long time due to being at work. We sat in the corner of the entry area and chatted.

I asked her if she'd ever lived in Texas. She said, "No, never." She seemed a little confused at the question. I told her my dad had told me that she did. Our conversation seemed a little guarded from each side. It was good, but not as good as I hoped it would be. Someone walked up and talked to my mom about work, she introduced me, and then said that she was so sorry, but she had to go back to work. I understood and hugged her goodbye.

After our meeting we didn't meet again. She sent a few letters to me, and Wanita was getting curious about who was sending me the letters. I knew I had to call off our correspondence because of the heat that I was starting to get. I sent my mom a letter that said hopefully someday I'll be able to contact her again, but it was getting too dangerous for her to send me any more letters.

I was both relieved and heartbroken at the same time when I mailed her that final letter. I was living at Dan and Wanita's and had nowhere else to go. I also was afraid if people found out I was talking to my mom, they would shun me out at the church. I liked my new life and didn't want to lose it. My girlfriend and I talked a lot about it. I didn't think I would lose her, but there was a chance her dad would make us break up if they found out.

I'm glad I had the chance to talk to my mom that day, but I think it may have caused more damage to us both in doing so. I felt after that, that I'd imposed on her and shouldn't have. It left me with more guilt.

My girlfriend was so supportive of me and so curious of my life stories. Her life had been so very different from mine that I found her family stories like a fairytale. We were married on January 26, 1990. I was nineteen years old, and she was seventeen. We were so young, but looking back at that time, we didn't know we were.

Our marriage has had its rocky times, I'm sure like most marriages, but I was still broken inside then, and didn't know how to trust her love. I think I feared that she would leave me if I allowed her into my heart, just like my mother had. She's been more than patient with me.

We had three sons and a couple of acres we made a home on. It was hard, those early years. I had a good job that was consistent but didn't pay that well. I was always looking for extra work to help make ends meet. I worked all the time. We grew a big garden and had chickens, pigs, and cows. It was the best life I could manage for them.

My wife and our kids were close to her family, but I always felt a little like an outsider. My father-in-law and I didn't gel. He'd told me when we'd gotten married that I would never be treated like family, because I wasn't his blood. Only my wife was blood to him and that broke my heart. I'd hoped to have a family to call my own. It didn't happen.

Dan and Wanita treated me like family (ish). I always felt that at any time, I'd be kicked out of the family if I made them mad or didn't jump through their hoops. They loved me in their own way I guess, but we weren't as close as you may have thought, if you'd been around me through those years.

My wife was always pushing me to be more involved in the church, by going to every event, every church meeting. I loved the smell of the church; it smelled like a library. I remember when I was young, when we did go to church, the smell and how it comforted me in an odd way. But I hated the social aspect of the church. I still wasn't good with conversation, and most of the time I would just stand there quietly and only speak if spoken to.

I was still trying to understand the language of being social. I watched and listened to everyone the best I could and tried to mimic those I thought I'd like to be like. Most of the time I felt stupid because people can tell when you're being fake.

When my wife and I were married, Dan gave me a list of about ten verses from the Bible to live our life by. Most of them were to hold up the traditions of the church, and there was no real context to them. Dan told me, "If we lived our lives according to the traditions, we would be all right."

I tried to fit into the crowd the best I could. I felt like I was a chameleon; constantly changing for whoever I was around. It was exhausting! There was all this pressure, and all the while, I was trying my best to forget my past. It would never fail at some church event, typically in a crowd of older men, one of them would bring up a story about my dad and how he'd either brought a Bible to church, or something else that would bring me shame in their eyes. I'd typically just say, "Yep, that's my dad," as I looked for the nearest exit. I never understood why they would do that. I think it was to make sure I stayed in my place at the bottom of the heap.

After several years, my dad's oldest brother and I started to be around each other. He played music and asked me to play with him in a family bluegrass band. I really wanted to... but didn't play an instrument. He mentioned they needed a dobro. I didn't know what that was, but went to the music store and bought one and started learning to play. A dobro is an acoustic steel slide guitar. Every Saturday evening was spent playing music with him and his son and grandsons.

It was the best time of my life up to that point. I had gotten older; I'd been married for years and had a young family. Life was now even better, my uncle was talking to me, and although I struggled with depression from time to time, life was good, my past was long ago.

Then there was a knock on my door.

20

◆

Knock, Knock...

My day was going well before I heard the knocking on my front door. I opened the door and there stood my dad. I froze as I looked at him. The first words he chose to say to me in eighteen years were, "Oh #$&! You got big!"

I'd spent the last ten years as a garbage hauler, back when you actually had to manually lift the cans into the truck. Dumping about a thousand cans a day tends to put muscle on you. After he said that, something snapped in me. I grabbed him by the shirt and said to him through clenched teeth, "WHAT ARE YOU DOING HERE!?"

I was so angry! Our house was a ranch style house with a covered porch, the front door right in the middle. I started pushing him in the chest, back towards the driveway as I yelled at him. Needless to say, I still had a lot of anger towards him.

Years before, I had received the brass buckle that he had beat me with in the mail. Just a box with the buckle in it. It made me so mad, but not as mad as it made my wife. She looked at it and then grabbed it out of my hand, taking it to the trash can. She flipped the lid open and threw it in with a thud, slamming the lid behind her. She was so angry!

Remember, my dad was a narcissist and that was his way of saying "Remember that day? I still have power over you...Fear me!"

I pushed my dad all the way to the driveway, and actually onto the hood of his car. He just kept saying, "Don't hit me! Don't hit me!" He then said something that caused me to pause in confusion.

He said, "I don't drink anymore. I got hypnotized and I don't drink or crave McDonald's french fries anymore."

What he'd said was so ridiculous that it stopped me in my tracks.

"WHAT?" I said. He said it again and then said, "I want to come back to the church, and you have to help me."

I was up against a wall in my mind. From what I knew of the church rules, family had to help if someone wanted to come back to the church. I was the only son, and both of my sisters were married. I didn't have a choice.

I told him I'll have to think about it and got his phone number to call him later. After he left, I felt like I'd fallen down inside and couldn't get back up. It was so strange. It was like a dam had started to break, letting all the bad memories get through. I started to have nightmares about the beatings, waking up in a cold sweat. I'd find myself out in the barn crying, struggling to stop. I was coming unraveled inside. I think I was having a nervous breakdown.

I went to my uncles and talked to them. They said I was up and it was my responsibility to help him. I talked to Dan, and he said the same thing. I felt trapped. I also could feel the pressure from people at the church to help him, but to keep him on a short leash, like I was responsible for what he said or where he went. It was horrible.

My uncle and his family slowly pulled away from me. Dan and his family did the same. My friends started to not come around, because my dad might be there, and they didn't want to be around him. My little sister even called me and yelled at me, telling me to,

"KEEP DAD AWAY FROM MY MOTHER!"

I told her, "He's your dad too! YOU tell him!"

She refused and just stopped talking to me completely. She's never forgiven me for my dad trying to visit her mother... It's so strange. I haven't talked to her now for more than twenty years and the Older Sister for about twenty-five years. They're both still full of hate for me, I think, because I escaped the crazy and moved on. At least, I thought I'd moved on... until Dad showed back up. Ugh!

Most people I was close to, had begun to distance themselves from me. It didn't seem to me that my dad had come back to go to church. I don't know why he was back. It seemed that he just came back to make a mess of my life. I think there had to have been an evil spirit involved in the whole thing. It was all really bad for my mind, and it totally broke me. I think God allowed it to happen for a reason, just like the rest of the things in my life. For what reason I didn't know.

I fell into a deep depression. In three months' time, I lost thirty pounds and then gained sixty-six pounds back. It was crazy to gain that much weight when I wasn't hardly eating anything. I was living on coffee and cigarettes. It made me scared that maybe I was sick inside. We couldn't go to the doctor, so I didn't know what to do. I prayed to God for help, but I can't say I could see Him working in the way I wanted at that time. I stopped smoking, thinking that might help. I felt better but got fatter as a consequence. Those were bad years.

My dad has a way with people. Some people love him, but with most people, he can really make you dislike him in a hurry. I think there's probably very few people, though, who dislike my dad as much as my wife does. She knew what I'd been through with him and what I now was going through trying to help him.

On this day, I had just pulled into the driveway, getting home from work. My dad's car was there. I thought, "Oh man, what's he doing here?" As I walked in, I saw him sitting at the dining room table. I also saw the look my wife gave me, as I walked in. I knew that look—she was, let's just say, very upset with the situation.

I asked my dad, "What's up? What are doing at my house without me here?"

There was a book on the table, he pushed it across the table to me. It was a cookbook. He said, "Your wife doesn't like to cook fish!" I looked and it was a book on how to cook fish. I knew now what was going on.

A couple of weeks back my dad wanted to take my sons fishing for trout. After much pressure I agreed, but only if my dad's youngest brother went with us. I needed a buffer. After we got home with a few fish, my dad thought my wife would be his slave and cook up all his fish for him. She wasn't going to be bullied and told him she doesn't cook fish!

OK, that's why he's at my house. It was a power move. He'd bought a cookbook so my wife would have to cook his fish the next time. I looked at him and slid the book back to him saying, "She knows how to cook fish; she just doesn't like to." I told him, "You need to leave."

He picked up his book and left. After that, we stopped talking for a few months. It was his way of punishing me for not bowing to his will. I wasn't going to be bullied by him anymore. It had gotten bad. He started to try and run my life with his bullying tactics.

During this time of silence, my dad went hunting and fell down as he was crossing a creek, landing on his back hard on a big rock. It collapsed his lung. He made his way to the hospital, and they operated on him without my knowledge.

I received a call from the Veteran's Hospital saying my dad was there, and the doctor needed to speak with me. The doctor said my dad couldn't stay at the hospital, and there was no one else to come and get him. He also said that if my dad stayed in the hospital, he would probably die from an infection due to his injuries.

I had to almost flip a coin to decide if I let him stay there and die or go and get him. OK… I didn't, but it was a hard choice for a few minutes.

I went up to see him and he had a very large chunk of his back missing. There was a hole that I could put my shoe in if I'd wanted to. I could see his rib bones and the stuff on the inside too. I stepped back and told the doctors, "Nope| I don't know what to do with that! Why is there a huge hole in my dad's back?"

They said that after his surgery there was a bad infection that had set in and that they had to cut it out. They were afraid of sepsis infection if he stayed in the hospital, and he'd have a better chance of living if he was at home. They told me a nurse would change his bandages in the morning at home and then I'd have to change them at night. They showed me how and sent a bunch of supplies home with us.

A nurse met us at my dad's house that first evening, to help get the process started. When the nurse first took off his bandages she gasped and called the doctor and freaked out on him. I knew then that this wasn't a normal situation. We had to fill the cavity with gauze that had been soaked in a solution. Then there were heavy strings, like shoelaces, glued to his skin on either side of the large wound. We would tie him shut and then wrap a clean bandage around him. They wanted the wound to heal from the inside out, so it wouldn't seal at the outside and rot inside. The old gauze had to be taken out and replaced every twelve hours.

We did this for three months until he was healed up. He was a jerk to me the entire time I tended to his wounds. Most nights I'd have to make his dinner too. The only way I could go back every evening was to put the hate I had for him in a box inside my heart and set it to the side. After he was healed up, I tried to not pick that box back up again. I still have a deep dislike for my dad, but the deep hate that was burning me up inside, I'm trying to not let it consume me anymore.

Only a few years later my dad would disappear from my life again. I thought good riddance, but I was still very broken and deeply depressed. I'd try once in a while and go for a walk on lunch break at work. Many times, I found myself walking across a bridge over the river, calling my wife and jokingly saying, "I'm on the bridge, and thinking about jumping." The only problem was, I wasn't joking. It was a cry for help. I was imploding under the pressure. Very dark days.

I tried hitting the gym every day, running on the treadmill like my past was chasing me. But I couldn't escape it.

21

◆

A Tearful Reunion

Shortly before my dad disappeared out of my life the second time, he called me and said my mom wanted to meet me and my family. I agreed and he said he would come too. I told him we didn't want him there. Begrudgingly he agreed, and a date was set to bring my family to meet my mom and her husband at a restaurant near their home.

I was so nervous on the way up to see them. The song "The Prayer" by Celine Dion came on the radio, and I started sobbing. I couldn't stop crying, I felt like a little kid that had just been found after being lost in the woods for a long time. Was she going to recognize me, now that I was in my thirties? Was she going to be nice to me or…I couldn't think how bad it would hurt if this went poorly. My wife just reached over and held my hand as I drove. No words needed. She was there with me and knew how hard this was going to be for us both.

My heart was racing out of my chest when we arrived at the restaurant. A car pulled up and there she was. My mom. I got out and walked up to her and said, "Mom?"

She said, "Yes," and she started to cry, grabbing me in an embrace that I can still feel.

"Mom, I've missed you and I'm sorry," I said.

She softly grabbed my face and said, "You have nothing to be sorry for! I'm the one who's to blame."

We stood there and cried hugging each other in the parking lot. Her husband said, "We can hug more after dinner, we have reservations." I think the whole thing had him very nervous. I don't blame him. He knew my dad and how narcissistic he was, but he didn't know me at all. Was I going to be like my dad? And he knew of the church rules. How was this going to hurt his wife if it all went poorly?

We had a great dinner getting to know each other again. It was a little nerve-racking, but really good at the same time. After dinner they invited us to their house for cookies. I told my mom I was like the cookie monster when it comes to cookies.

She laughed and said she was too! "You must get that from me!" she said with a big smile.

We got to their house, and it was a very nice house in a gated community. My dad had never stopped showing up and bugging her. They'd had to move to a gated community to try and keep him away. I think he still thought of my mom as his property.

We went in and had cookies; she had a big assortment to choose from. She had me sit on the couch as she went and got a big pile of photo albums. My mom had suffered with Multiple Sclerosis and her feet had also been damaged in a bad car accident after she'd stopped seeing us. She had trouble walking. I wanted her to sit next to me on the couch, but she sat at my feet on the floor showing me pictures of her life and telling me all about it. I thought it was great. I couldn't get enough. My wife told me later, "It was really sad to watch."

What a great night, but sadly we had to go home. I can still see my mom standing at the door, wringing her hands in distress, like she wasn't ever going to see me again. I think her heart was breaking as she hugged me one last time before I had to go. It was so hard to leave her standing there. She kept apologizing for the life I'd had. I hadn't told her about the abuse, but she knew there had been some. I don't think she knew how bad it had really been. I kept telling her not to be sorry. "Let's just enjoy each other now," I said.

We emailed and sent letters and cards. Sometimes it would be a while between the letters, and it made me nervous, but we kept in touch a little. I wanted her in my life full time, but the Lord had other plans.

We, again, started to drift away from each other. The letters and cards became fewer and fewer, and the distance between them got further and further apart. Then my mom's husband sent me a letter, blaming us for the pain my mom had been through and not continuing to pursue the relationship. I'm sure my mom didn't know he had sent it. It hurt my wife and me that he was angry with us, but at that time we didn't know how to fix it. We were so stuck in the church that it felt impossible to have both my mom and please the Followers' rules.

I think God was here as well in my story. Not because of the church, but because of what was to come. Looking back, I think God may have allowed me to continue to be broken and was allowing my life to spiral to rock bottom. Rock bottom is what He would build His foundation on. Don't think this can't happen. Don't think God wouldn't allow you to fall down and implode, only to rebuild you after. Read about Job in the Bible.

A few years passed with only a letter once in a while from each of us. My mom's health started to take a bad turn, and she disappeared off the radar for a couple of years without any contact. She finally sent me an email explaining that she'd been very sick with her MS, and it had taken its toll even worse than before.

Her birthday was coming up and I asked her if I could take her to dinner. I also asked if it could be just her and me, without any outside stress of people. I asked her to make sure it was OK with her husband first. I knew he didn't care for our dipping into his life every few years. I can't blame him for it, I'm sure it was very confusing to him.

She agreed and I picked her up and we went to a nice restaurant. She looked bad. She looked like she'd been very ill for a very long time. She sat next to me at the table and held my hand, saying, "This time we'll get it right."

She brought a book of her family tree with her. It was full of information that I never knew about her family. We looked through the book while we ate a great dinner. She would stop the waitresses and tell them I was her son. She was so proud of me that night. It made her happy and it made me blush. We talked and talked for hours. We asked hard questions of each other, and it was OK.

The conversation we had that night needed to happen. It wasn't emotional. We weren't crying or mad. I had questions and so did she. I wondered if normal people have conversations like this with their mothers. It was getting late, and we had to say goodbye. I thanked her husband and shook his hand. It was a happy goodbye, and he could tell this time seemed different.

This time we stayed in touch. We planned a BBQ at our house

when the weather got warmer. My sons and their wives were OK with meeting her and her husband. I had a few months of peace in the storm.

I didn't care if the church found out about us. I'd been questioning the traditions of the church in my heart for a while now. I was becoming disillusioned with the church. Years before, my sister-in-law died in childbirth, and it tore a hole in me that they wouldn't go to the hospital. Then several little kids started getting sick and dying, and that made me mad.

I asked Dan, "Does the Bible really say that we shouldn't go to the hospital and if it does, where? "

He just barked at me saying, "It's in there, stop questioning it."

I didn't read the Bible very often and felt intimidated when I would try. I couldn't seem to make sense of any of it. I don't think Dan read much either. When questioned about the Bible he would say, "I'll have to call an older man in the church to ask his opinion on this or that," never what the Bible actually said. With each death I felt like I was further and further from the truth.

It was in May 2016, just a couple weeks away from our planned BBQ, when my mom's husband called me at work. He told me he had just heard from a friend that my mom had passed out while at the store, and they took her to the hospital. He couldn't get her on the phone and couldn't leave work right then either. He asked me if I could go and see what was going on and call him. He told me the name of the hospital.

I said, "That hospital is just across the street from my office, I'll go over right away and let you know what I find out in a few minutes."

I went over to the hospital and asked the front desk where my mom's room was. They told me and I headed up to see her. I knocked on the door and went in. My mom was there, and she was so happy to see me. She said that she'd passed out at the store and woke up here. The doctors were running some tests to find out why.

I called her husband and handed my mom the phone. They spoke for a few minutes, my mom reassuring him she was OK. The doctor soon came in, followed by the chaplain. I thought, "This can't be good."

The doctor told my mom he was very sorry, but the tests found that she was full of cancer. She had cancer in her lungs, liver, and pancreas. He also told her that, sadly, she only had about six months to live.

She took the news so well. She was calm and asked a few questions about what her next moves were. Her mind was spinning... my heart was breaking. Our lives had just started to mend after a lifetime of tearing us apart. Now she was going to leave me again, but this time, for good.

My wife and I decided to be in her life as much as we could until the end, not caring who knew or what they might say. My mom and her husband came over for the BBQ at our house. All of our sons and their wives were there too. It was a great day.

My wife and I went to her house as many times as we could in the next few months. My mom had great conversations with me, as well as with my wife. I got to know her husband too. He's a good man and really loved my mom. I thanked him for being so good to her all these years, and for giving me another chance to be in their lives.

"It was all water under the bridge," he said. "Let's enjoy what we have now while we have it."

My mom liked to play card games on the patio soaking in the summer sun. It was so fun playing with her. She had a great sense of humor, and we'd banter back and forth. During those times I'd often think, "What would my life had looked like if I'd went with her and not my dad? Is this what having a mom feels like to everyone? If yes, how lucky everyone is!"

We would sometimes just sit and drink tea in the shade, I'd sit there quietly listening to her tell me all about her life. I soaked it all in, trying to remember every word. That's how I knew about the beginning of this book. Hard stories, but needed stories to fill in the blanks I had. Through it all, she would always tell me one thing over and over. She'd say to me, "The most important thing you need to know about me is, I'm a Christian."

I didn't understand what she meant when she said that. I thought, "OK, you were a good woman and didn't do bad things." I had no idea what she was saying to me at that time. I'd tell her, "That's good, Mom."

She was so patient with me, just smiling back at me. But when the chance arose again later, she would drop it into our conversations. I think she was testing where I was in my walk with the Lord. I hadn't told her about the time I'd prayed for the snow, or why I needed to. I hadn't told her about the abuse I'd suffered at the hands of The Stepmother. I didn't want to break her heart. She already carried so much guilt that she wasn't there for most of my life. I didn't want to make it worse for her. We just avoided the conversation, except when she had a question, or I did, on something specific that I was trying to put together in my mind.

She slowly started to get sicker and sicker. It was so hard to watch, but I wouldn't have missed it for anything. We were making up for so much lost time. She couldn't sit on the porch anymore; it was too hard for her to be outside. It seemed like the transition from her chair in the living room to her not getting out of bed was really fast. My wife and one of our daughters-in-law went up to her house often, to help her with whatever was needed. I'm glad they had that time with her. She was slowly drifting away as the cancer took its toll. It broke my heart seeing her in pain.

The last conversation I had with my mom was wonderful, and a gift from God, I think. I'm so thankful I was able to get to know her. The precious time we had together was short, the beginning of my life, and the end of hers, but every moment I will cherish forever. My mom died November 23, 2016.

I love you Mom, and I miss you very much.

22

But God

My mom's passing was the straw that broke me completely. I fell into a deep depression. I just didn't care about anything anymore. I started to drink heavily to try and numb my mind. I was falling headfirst towards rock bottom. There was so much going on at the church that I thought was crazy, and that didn't help matters either. I felt like I needed to escape it all, but didn't know what to do. I started looking for property in Alaska to run away to, thinking that would help. I knew my wife and kids wouldn't follow me and in my depressed state, I almost didn't care. Rock bottom was close, and I knew when I hit it, it was going to hurt really bad or kill me.

My wife pushed me to go to church every meeting and if I didn't, she let me know how unhappy she was with me. I felt like she didn't understand what I was going through, and we weren't communicating very well during this time either. I felt like she'd stopped loving me, wanting me to leave. I'm sure my drinking and bad temper wasn't helping. I'd go to church just to not have to hear her grump at me.

We'd go to church every Thursday and Sunday as was our traditional schedule. We didn't have any ministry at the church. Remember, the last pastor died in 1969, six months before I was born. The last elder died when I was fifteen years old. Since 1986, our church service was only singing ten hymns with a short silent prayer during the service, no Scripture being read and no preaching. After singing the same few hymns for the last twenty-five years, you tend to just drone through them, not singing with any understanding or much care. I was just going through the motions trying to keep it together the best I could, failing most of the time, until finally I hit rock bottom with a splat! That's when God showed up.

It was a Thursday in June 2017. I'd been sitting there at church, droning away on some hymn. I heard a rustle in the crowd that caused me to look up. Three men had walked in from the back room and were walking up onto the pulpit.

Now you need to understand a few things, for this interaction to really make sense. The church had basically been closed off from the outside world for almost fifty years. Very few people, if any, ever visited the church that weren't members, and on the rare occasion a stranger tried to attend, they wouldn't be welcome. But on this day, those men didn't seem to care about our rules. They walked up onto the pulpit and people freaked out!

The pulpit was a type of holy ground, if you will. People would rarely go up there, and it was weird when you did. You were able to go up there when you got married or on a very special occasion. If a little kid was running around up there after the church service was over, they would get in trouble from their mother.

The three men were there to give us a message, one of them said, into the microphone, before it was hurriedly turned off. Only one of the men spoke, with the other two looking more like bodyguards. The man doing the talking said, "I feel like God has put a message on my heart to tell you. I'm not here to be your pastor, only to give the message and then I will leave."

People were standing and yelling for him to get down from there. Women were rushing up to grab their children from where they were sitting near the front of the sanctuary, covering their children's ears while rushing them out the side doors. The sanctuary is very large, holding about 2,000 people. That night there weren't a lot of people there, possibly 1,200 or so. It was total chaos.

Older men were yelling at these men to get down from the pulpit and go into the backroom area of the church. This area is very large as well. There's a large kitchen with a large fellowship space where all the social events take place. The visitors agreed, and all the men in the church followed them into the backroom.

"Only men went to hear them?" you might ask. Yep, only men. At the Followers church, women are second class citizens, and they need to stay in their place, and their place isn't with the men when things have to be discussed. I certainly don't agree with that thinking now, if you're wondering.

So, all the men went in the back to hear what he had to say. The man was standing there in the middle of the room. I was about fifteen feet away from him. He was just standing there quietly with a Bible open in his hand. I watched as men yelled at him, taking turns getting in his face like a swarm of bees. I saw a man from the church standing there, pulling at his hair, yelling at the top of his lungs for the visiting men to get out. But nothing was going to detour him from his quest. He wasn't leaving until he gave his message.

The scene was pure confusion. Finally, a man named Jason stepped out of the crowd and yelled, "Everyone shut up! I want to hear what he has to say!" Everyone quieted down.

I thought, "Wow! That was brave."

The visiting man said again, "I feel like God has put a message on my heart to give you all. You've forgotten what grace is. You've forgotten what Jesus did on the cross."

I was confused. Grace? What's grace? I knew Jesus was God's Son and He died on the cross, but so what? I didn't understand. What's he talking about? Grace... what's grace? All of a sudden, I felt sick inside, and I then had a deep hunger to find out what he was talking about. Jesus and grace. I didn't know what this all meant, but I needed to find out!

The man then read something out of his Bible. I can't remember what it was. He answered a couple questions on his calling to ministry. One man from the crowd asked if he was a preacher? The visiting man said, "Yes, I'm a pastor." Then he was asked if he'd went to school to learn how to be a pastor and how to read the Bible? He said, "Yes, I've been to seminary." The crowd all moaned in disgust.

"If you went to school to learn the Bible, you're a phony," they said. The pastor disagreed with them, having a back-and-forth semi-heated discussion. Then he closed his Bible and just left with the other two men who had come with him. I stood there in a daze. I had questions that needed to be answered, but as I looked around, there was no one I felt I could talk to about it. All of the men were in a buzz, talking the pastor down as a phony.

I was spun and alone. I made my way to the car where my wife was. She asked, "What did the man say?"

I told her, "He said we've forgotten what grace is and what Jesus did on the cross... I think we need to find out what he's talking about."

She said, "I think so too."

When I got home that day, I Googled "grace" to find out what it meant. Google said, "Biblical grace is the basis for the Christian faith. God's grace is defined as unmerited favor. Grace cannot be earned; it is something that is freely given by the Lord."

Grace was something I'd never heard of before. It went against everything I'd been taught at the church. "Works" is what I knew got you into heaven. Hopefully, you'd do enough "works," and add a coin, as it were, to your bag of "works" you could give to God at the end of your life. I always pictured it like standing before God holding that bag up saying, "Here's the payment for what's owed!" and hope it was enough to get me into heaven.

This grace... was something new. Unmerited favor? Salvation was a free gift given? I was struggling to understand the concept. Who could I talk to about grace and works?

At work I had an employee who everyone knew was a Christian. He didn't push his faith on anyone or get offended if someone said something off. He just let his light shine in this dark world. His name is Tim. I thought, "I'll ask Tim when I get to work the next day, I bet he'll have the answers I need!"

At the start of shift the next morning, I asked Tim if I could talk with him in the meeting room. He looked nervous. "What's this about?" he asked when I shut the door.

I said, "I have a question I hope you can help me with." I asked, "To get into heaven, is it by doing good works, or is it grace?" He actually laughed at me for a second, I think he thought I was messing with him. When I said, "No, I'm serious," he realized I wasn't kidding, and I really wanted to know.

Tim said, "It's all about grace, you can't buy your way into heaven!" I told him, "OK, we need to talk." I asked him so many questions. He was so patient and answered what he could. We talked at lunch most days the next week and again the week after. Actually, I think we talked several times a week for the next five years. I had so many questions and so much baggage I needed help working through.

Thank you Tim, for your advice, patience, and friendship. Our conversations have been a gift from the Lord. He knew I needed someone to help me find my way into this new world that He had set before me.

I understood grace was a real thing. My mind was spinning. "What now? If grace is true, and we couldn't earn our salvation by works, then what else had we been taught that wasn't true either?"

About a week after the Lord opened my eyes to grace, there was another church function. I was standing in my group, at the other end of the back porch at the church that evening. Remember, I was raised differently and didn't really understand how everything worked at the church, especially when it came to the social aspects of things. I never felt I could walk up to a group of men and just be a part of their group. I know…that's weird, especially if you, the reader, are from the church too. Regardless, that's how I felt. If I did approach a group, I always felt out of place unless invited. I saw the church structure as factions. I would typically just stand there and observe everyone and their interactions.

From my perspective, it seemed there was a slide scale of where you were in the order of things. If you were popular and/or wealthy, you were near the top of the scale. If you were a little different or came from the wrong family, you're at the bottom. It was difficult to move up in the ranks, in my opinion, unless you started to make a lot of money. People seemed to like you more if you had money, even if you were a jerk. Actually, it seemed it was a requirement, if you were at the top to be an arrogant jerk to us at the bottom. Money and your place on the scale, that's how I saw it. Hopefully, that explanation should help with the next part of the story. Why I didn't feel like I could just "jump factions" as it were, without first being asked to join them. Hopefully, that makes sense.

OK, back to the story…It was just a few days from the pastor's visit. I'd talked to my friend at work and now I was at the church for a party of some kind, I can't remember what it was for. I was standing there with my people that I normally stood with, listening to them talk about how great they golfed and how big their new pickup truck was. I was so bored with their conversation. I just didn't care about the things they were talking about. I was looking across the back porch at a group of men standing in the corner.

I knew of these men, most of them were about ten years younger than I was and thought of by many in the church as Zealots—people who appeared to know more about Scripture than what we considered "normal." I'd been around them very little; at a graduation party at one of their homes, I sat there and listened as they passionately argued with each other about what one verse in the Bible meant. They were often labeled as "exalted" by most people in the church, and they were a group I tried my hardest to steer clear of.

As I stood there in my regular group, I couldn't help but think, "I wonder what *they* are talking about?" I was being drawn to these men and I didn't know why. I made my way over towards them. When I got close to where they were standing, I started to just kind of inch over closer a little at a time. I remember Jason giving me an odd look as I was getting nearer to them. Jason later told me he thought I was crazy wanting to stand with them. Didn't I know that he was now hated by the church?

Jason was the man who stepped out of the crowd, telling everyone to shut up, when the pastor visited our church. But, at the time, I thought the odd look from Jason was because I wasn't one of their group. I finally got the courage to stand with them. They were talking about the pastor and what he'd said. It seemed to me they were spun by his visit like I was. These guys were known as ones who read the Bible. I'd never really read the Bible very much, so I just listened to what they were saying. I was trying to figure out what they were talking about and also hoping they wouldn't ask me any questions.

My recollection of what God did, and how we were moved, might be a little different than others' memories of the story. Remember, this is my story and how I saw it. If you have five people, and they all see the same car accident, each will have a slightly different account of the event. This might be a little like that, but God's story is what I want you to focus on as you read on. We would all agree, we want to give God the glory in all of it, because it wasn't anything we did except follow when He called to us.

With that being said, we could do nothing BUT follow His call, so again, it was all God and to Him be all the glory!

23

A Bouquet of Brothers

I had successfully jumped factions and felt alive again. The darkness that I'd been trapped in was still there, but there was now a light that was taking my focus away from the darkness. God was on the move, it seemed, and we were being drawn towards a Light and a life we never saw coming.

I'd been quietly standing by these men at church, just listening to them talk over a couple of weeks. I didn't really know them well yet, but my first impression was that I found them very interesting and very passionate about their convictions. The men I knew them to be before, didn't seem to be the men that were there before me now.

I'm going to introduce you, one by one, to these men. Jason, Brad, Marshall, Luke, Mark, Casey, Justin, and Gary. There were others that came and went, but these men were the core of my new brothers in Christ.

First, let me introduce Jason, the one who stood up to the crowd the day the pastor came out to the Followers' church. He was the one who said, "Let him speak!" I got the impression that Jason wouldn't back down from a fight, and I respected that about him. Jason seemed to be in a heated conversation most of the time, with many in the group, but I think he was trying to get us to think about all the different angles and not get stuck in the past.

Next there was Brad. I felt the most comfortable around him because

I'd known him the longest, due to our kids being friends. He talked way over my head most of the time, but I felt he was sincere in his convictions.

Then there was Marshall. I only knew of him. I don't think I'd ever spoken to him before I started standing with the group. He's a deep thinker, and I noticed if he didn't agree with you, he'd laugh a little, and then give a well thought through rebuttal. He's also the historian of the group, and he's really good at it.

Now onto Luke. He's very charismatic, but not in a "Pentecostal" way. What I mean by that is, he is good with people, and they're drawn to him. He has an ability to make people feel valued and heard. He does this with such ease, never making someone feel less or stupid for asking a question. He's also very good at hiding how incredibly intelligent he is.

That brings us to Mark. Mark was like a social butterfly. I'd observed him landing shortly with a group out at the church for a quick visit, then off to another group, just like a butterfly in a field of flowers, keeping his finger on the pulse of the church. You could always tell where he was by his infectious laugh. His ability to remember and quote verses from the Bible has always had me in awe. Little did I know at the time, he would go on to become one of the closest friends that I've ever had.

And then there was Casey. He was a deep thinker and very passionate about his convictions.

Next is Justin. He has a booming voice and the ability to mediate in time of conflict within the group. The only way you can tell he's getting heated, or upset is his voice gets a bit louder for a second before turning back to sound reasoning. His ability to "iron out the wrinkles" in the group isn't something that's taught, it's a gift.

Then there's Gary. God has a funny way of using people in your life. Some people God uses to lead you in a certain direction. Others, He uses to break you down to where He wants you. Then there are some, that God uses to show you His power and glory. Gary happens to be one of those people that God used in my journey in this way.

Gary was someone I'd known from afar. I knew him as a difficult person that was very angry and very hard to be around. I saw him as stubborn and without any kindness or love in the way he spoke to most people. I wasn't close to Gary, and we didn't have very many interactions, if at all, but I would watch him in the crowd. He was a person I tried to stay as far away from as possible.

After a couple of weeks standing with these guys at church, my wife and I were invited to Marshall's house by Brad. We thought, "Maybe we wouldn't go." It felt weird being invited to someone's house by someone else. Then we were also invited by Casey. "OK," we thought, "since we'd been invited twice, maybe we should go."

We went and we were so nervous! We went into the house, and we were met by Jennifer, Marshall's wife. She treated us like we were old friends, she was so welcoming. The men were all outside by the campfire and the women were inside. I went out to the fire and sat down. A few of the guys were already sitting around the fire. They were in a deep conversation about their thoughts on grace and what it really meant.

I was being quiet as usual, just listening, then Gary sat down next to me. I thought "Oh, great, here we go. Should I move?" All the seats were taken, I had no choice, I had to stay where I was.

Then something happened that I never saw coming. Gary started to talk, and what he said and how he said it was so different. The angry, difficult man I knew before was gone. As Gary spoke, I was drawn into his words about grace. He spoke about God's love and what that looked like. He was so patient as he listened to my questions and didn't make me feel stupid about my ignorance of what the Bible really said. I had a lot of baggage that was clouding my understanding, but that was OK. Gary and the others were so kind and showed me what the love of Christ should look like.

"Love is patient and kind; love does not envy or boast; it is not arrogant or rude. It does not insist on its own way; It is not irritable or resentful; it does not rejoice at wrongdoing but rejoices with the truth. Love bears all things, believes all things, hopes all things, and endures all things." 1 Corinthians 13:4-7

These men were changed, and I felt I was being changed as well. I think the Holy Spirit took a hold of me that night, there by the fire with my new brothers. I told Gary, "To me he looked like an old tree with new leaves." I actually have a picture of an old tree with new leaves and light shining through it as Gary's contact picture when he calls my cell phone. The men helped me set up a WhatsApp on my phone so I could be in contact with them in a new group text.

We all seemed to have different personalities, strengths, and weaknesses. It was like God was gathering wildflowers from His field, each completely different, but the same. As He pulled us together, we made His bouquet. Our eyes were being opened, and our hearts were being changed. God was doing something in us we couldn't explain. I wasn't looking for Jesus the day He sent that pastor to our church. I didn't even know who Jesus really was, but

He knew me. He knew us, and it seemed He had a task for us to do. It grew late and we had to go home. When we went to leave, my wife and I just sat in our car, in the driveway. We sat there for about a half an hour and cried. It was so strange and so wonderful at the same time. That night I didn't feel the darkness like before. I felt a peace inside and a hunger to know more about the Lord. If you've never been reborn, I hope you get to. It's the most wonderful feeling I've ever experienced.

After that night, the group gathered together two or three times a week. We were on fire for the Lord and couldn't get enough. Some in our group had been saved a few years before and were still hiding in the darkness of the church. We all seemed to be at different stages in our walk with the Lord. I was like a newborn baby Christian, I knew nothing. But God...

He put us all together for a reason and put blinders on us to keep our eyes looking forward towards Him and towards grace. Once you see grace you can't unsee it. Grace draws you towards the Lord. Grace calls for you to follow regardless of the cost, and follow we did.

First, we would have deep conversations that went on for hours and hours. Then the Lord brought us sermons. I can't say I'd ever listened to a sermon before. Some in the group had grown up with their families listening to Billy Graham on TV. Others had been secretly listening to sermons on the radio. Luke had been saved for a few years by then. God, it seemed, had him in a holding pattern until He was ready to gather us together and use him.

Luke had found an app on his phone called Sermon Audio. He

shared the app with us and oh man! Things started to take off. Mark sent me the first sermon I'd ever listened to. It was called, "Salvation by Works, a Criminal Doctrine" by Charles Spurgeon. I was so scared to listen to it. Was this stepping out too far? Was I ready to really follow the Lord? Did I know enough about the Bible to listen to a sermon from someone outside of our church? I had so much baggage and ignorance. Mark encouraged me to set aside my fears and listen to it. I finally did, and…it wrecked me!

I was so convicted. I cried. It was like I could feel the stony heart being ripped out of me with each word. I felt like everything I had believed in, everything I had ever been taught, was a lie. Sometimes God shows you things gradually and sometimes He chooses to hit you between the eyes with truth. And hit me He did. I needed to know more of the truth I'd just heard. I felt like I was, all of a sudden, starving for truth, starving for the Word. I think we all were feeling the same way.

God had lit a fire in us that wasn't going to be extinguished. My second sermon I listened to was William Hughes' sermon called "Blessed are the Meek." As I listened, I felt like I'd been plugged in, being charged like a battery. It felt like God had reached inside of me and turned on a light. A light that was slowly being turned up, making it brighter and brighter. We were all that way, starving for more, starving for the Word. Sermons were flying back and forth through the text group on WhatsApp. We would listen to thirty to fifty sermons a week. We couldn't get enough.

I found a Christian radio station that played sermons. I was at work making my rounds, visiting my crews in the field, and I really enjoyed listening to whatever new pastor who might be speaking that hour. I turned on the radio this day and the pastor had a great Scottish accent. Alistair Begg is his name. As I listened to his sermon on Psalm 22, my mind was blown. I never knew what a Psalm was, and I was so surprised at how interesting I found it. Then more pieces started to fall into place, and I thought, "That sounds like Jesus on the cross…I think Psalm 22 is talking about Jesus on the cross!" My mind was spinning on how the Psalm was written hundreds of years before Jesus was born, and it was talking about Jesus on the cross!

I had to pull over and through tears, I started calling my new brothers telling them to turn on the radio station and listen to this sermon on this Psalm 22 thing. I'm sure they thought I was crazy calling them all excited, or maybe it was a bit funny to them how I had no idea what a Psalm was. That's OK, I didn't care. They needed to hear this sermon.

I was taught to stay out of the Old Testament and Revelation. I was so surprised that the Old Testament talked about Jesus and the Cross. I didn't understand that the Old and New Testaments were one book. How can you know who God is if you never read the Old Testament? I slowly started to understand that the Old Testament pointed forward to the Cross, and the New Testament pointed back to the Cross. It's all about Jesus and his redemptive plan for us.

Remember when I was a boy and found that little red Bible? I knew somewhere in that book I could find God. I was right! To be honest, I kind of miss that excitement of new belief and discovering what God was opening my eyes and heart to.

Some—OK, most—of the sermons were way over my head, and

most of the time I was just trying to figure out where they were teaching in the Bible, and what was the context of the teaching. I liked listening to Allister Begg and I really liked Chuck Swindoll. Chuck Swindoll was like listening to your grandpa tell you a story.

Someone told me about John MacArthur, so I found one of his sermons and turned it on. After a few minutes I had to turn it off. He scared me. I wasn't ready to be blasted like that (LOL), but after a while I couldn't get enough of his "Hit you with the truth" teaching.

Then there was R.C. Sproul. R.C.'s the master in my opinion. No one can teach the Bible like R.C. can. It's like he takes you by the hand and leads you as you step into the pages of the Bible. It's like you're walking through the words as if it were a rose garden of fragrant flowers, each word more fragrant than the last. He teaches in an understandable way that not only baby Christians can understand, but seasoned ones as well. R.C.'s teaching seems to get deeper every time you listen to it, like it matures with you, easy for a baby to digest, and as you grow with Christ and are ready for meat, the same sermon turns into a carnivore's dream. I think you can listen to the same R.C. sermon every year and learn something new, like it grows with you. God was feeding us with wonderful teaching. Wonderful pastors who loved the truth and the Bible, but more importantly loved the Lord.

This went on for about five months, fire hose learning, at least on my part. It probably wasn't a healthy way to start out learning, but I was like a starving kid in a candy store, gorging on whatever I could devour.

24

The Bible Study

Grace was the wrecking ball that had smashed through the dam, releasing so many new ideas, so many new terms and words. At times I felt I would drown, having so much baggage from the way we'd been taught. It was like rocks in my pockets, not allowing me to come up for air, until I dropped them, one by one.

We talked about grace to great depths and listened to hundreds of sermons. But what should we do next?

What about doing a Bible study?

A WHAT?... A Bible study?!

We can't do that. A Bible study is against the "unwritten" rules of the church. This could get us into big trouble. Also, what does a Bible study even look like? We'd never seen one before. We went to Google and looked it up. It seemed to be self-explanatory.

We started talking about if we should, and if we did, were we stepping out too far from our traditions? One of the guys said that he'd seen a billboard out in front of a church in the area, that said it was having a Bible study on Saturday mornings.

"OK… you and you, go to the Bible study and get any papers they might have that we might need. Be sure to take some money, just in case, if they charge for it."

Others in our group said they knew of more churches in the area with studies going that they could visit too. "OK! Team up and go!"

It felt very clandestine, and so exciting! Doing a Bible study was breaking "rules," but going to a Bible study at another church would have been unforgivable.

The teams returned with their papers in hand. Each team reported with enthusiasm. The studies were fantastic, and it didn't cost us any money either!

We couldn't wait to get together and talk about what they'd experienced. We studied the paperwork they brought back and looked on the Internet at other study ideas as well. We discussed all the options over and over until we decided to vote on one.

"If we are going to do a Bible study, I better go and buy a new Bible," I thought. One of the guys had a thick Study Bible. I'd never seen anything like it. "I have to get one," I thought. I had an older Bible that was given to me by Dan before I got married, but it was just the New Testament.

In our discussion, we had decided to study the entire Bible. The Old Testament, New Testament, and Revelation. To be honest, I was nervous to read the New Testament, but the thought of reading the Old Testament had me scared. But Revelation... Dan had put such a fear in me about the Book of Revelation, that it had me completely petrified to even open the Bible to it.

Some in our group had grown up being able to read the Old and New Testaments, and even Revelation. It wasn't a big deal to them reading it at all. But I bet if you asked most people out at the Followers Church, they'd say that they were told by their parents or grandparents to stay out of the Old Testament and Revelation, because of two reasons. The first reason was, without Walter (the preacher who had died in 1969) leading us, there'd be no way for us to understand what was in the Bible. The second is that Walter taught from the pulpit to stay out of Revelation because we couldn't understand it, and it would just confuse us.

I've heard so many older men in the church say that exact thing, but again, some families read it all and some didn't. The group I was raised around didn't read the Bible at all it seemed, only the verses that shored up the traditions of the church.

As soon as I could, I went to the Christian bookstore, and WOW, there were so many Bibles to choose from. After probably an hour of looking and several calls to Luke for advice, I found one that I liked. I had my first Study Bible, and I was so proud of my new treasure. I sent pictures to all the guys with a, "look what I just got!"

The text group came alive with "Congratulations!" and "I can't wait to see it in person!" Having these new brothers was such a fantastic gift from the Lord. Who else would be just as excited as I was about buying a new Bible? No one I'd known before, but my new brothers were. Then it was like we were new fathers showing off pictures of our newborn children. Pictures of new Bibles started popping up in the feed. Each photo met with as much excitement as the previous and how we couldn't wait until next Saturday when we would start our study! We were all going to meet at Brad's house, and we couldn't wait.

The day of the study, I woke up early with the excitement of a child on Christmas morning. Saturday was finally here! I sprang out of bed and jumped into the shower, grabbed a cup of coffee and a bite to eat. I was ready to go, but it was still dark outside. Well... I was a few hours early and I had to wait. It was like being tortured sitting there watching the clock slowly tick away. I gently thumbed through my new Study Bible looking at everything.

At the store there were markers you could use to highlight verses in your Bible. I thought "NEVER! How could you write inside such a treasure like this?" I turned each page with the gentleness of a father wiping a tear from a newborn baby's face, so careful not to put a crease in any of the pages. I marveled at it, knowing we could find God in this book, and it seemed He was calling for me to do just that.

Time seemed to slow to a crawl as I waited to leave to Bible Study. Each tick of the clock making my heart jump with anticipation. How far was Brad's house? If I drove slow and maybe stopped and got some gas… I'd still be an hour early. Ugh!

Finally! After an eternity it seemed, it was time to go. I gently placed my new Bible back into the box it came in and then kissed my wife goodbye. I was as giddy as a schoolboy heading out for his first day of school. One by one all of my new brothers showed up with their new treasures in hand. Pages had been printed off from the study course we'd chosen. The Book of Philippians was going to be where God started our journey towards Him.

As we started our study, we could do nothing but cry. It wasn't like we opened our Bibles, and we were suddenly all knowing. Nope, not at all. The Holy Spirit was filling us with Living Water, and like a waterfall, it just poured out of our eyes in the form of tears. I'm not sure how many questions we got through that first day, it doesn't really matter. What does matter is this: The Lord had started a fire in us that wouldn't be quenched. A hunger to know more about our Savior. I was shocked to see Jesus everywhere I looked in the Bible. If and when I'd read the Bible before, to me, it was like Jesus kept getting in the way of seeing God in the story. Now things were different. The more we read the more we could see it's all about Jesus. The Old Testament points forward to the cross, and the New Testament points back to the cross. It's all about Jesus and what He did on the cross to save us from our sins.

Bible study was the best day ever! Even if I was bleeding to death, I would have still made it to study on Saturday mornings. It was a time of learning about the Lord, and a time to learn how to be a Christian. We learned how to pray in a corporate style. "OK, how about you open in prayer, and I'll close?" That seemed to work great! "So, let's do it that way each time."

Each of us were, I'd say, more of the type A personality, so the evil spirits used that against us every time they could. Pride, stubbornness, and old rivalries within the group seemed to rear their ugly heads way too often. But God... He kept us coming back with love towards each other.

The depression and darkness I'd struggled with for so long was used against me as well. I didn't realize at the time that I was struggling with PTSD from the horrors of my childhood. My dad's return had broken me, and I was really struggling to keep myself together. It was like light on one side of me and darkness on the other. I was losing the battle with the darkness and needed help.

After study one morning, I went to my car and couldn't seem to drive away. Brad, Luke, and Gary were still in the house and something within me pushed me back towards them. I dragged my feet as I went back into the house to where they were. Brad looked surprised and asked if I was OK. I said no. I was so afraid to share my past with my new brothers. Maybe I thought they would reject me, or think less of me? I don't know, but I was so afraid to lose them. The devil seemed to have buried that dart of fear deep within me.

I said to the guys, "I need help. I can't do this alone anymore." I told them of my struggles and a high-level overview of the abuse. Luke pulled his hat over his eyes as he listened with tears running down his face. Gary looked at his feet, leaning against the cabinet having to hold himself up, wiping a tear from his eye. Brad looked like he wanted to hug me as he listened, his eyes full of tears as well.

After I told my story, I asked them if they would please pray for me to have the strength I needed to just get through each day. Each prayed a prayer with more love than I'd ever known. A prayer for a brother in need. A prayer that I would look to the Lord for my strength, and to them when I needed a brother in those dark days to hold me up.

Don't ever underestimate the power of prayer, or the love of people who care about you. For me, I needed both. Although I would still struggle with my past until further into this story, the darkness that had been consuming me was pushed back for a time after that day my brothers prayed for me. I no longer felt like I was being pulled in half, in a struggle between darkness and light.

Spiritual warfare was still something we all had to be very careful not to fall to. I've heard, "Where the Lord is working, the devil is lurking," and we found that to be true. Each of us had something in our lives that the powers of evil were trying to distract us with.

Each week went by so slowly. Would Saturday ever get here? Our studies would go on for four to five hours sometimes. The only thing limiting our time was that we each had things we needed to go do each day. It was such a wonderful time, diving deep into the Bible.

Christmas was coming soon, and we decided to have a Christ-centered Christmas party at Brad's house. Each family put their name into a hat, and we drew names for gifts. The gift could be bought, but if you could make something faith based, that would be better. Some of our kids put on a Christian talent show. They did a skit, and they sang and played their instruments too. It was wonderful!

Before that year, Christmas, for most of us, was all about a fat man in a red suit. Not this year! We sang hymns together, we ate a meal together, we gave gifts of love to one another. It was the best Christmas I'd ever had. God was adding to His bouquet and pulling us closer together.

After a few months of the men doing our Bible study, we realized our wives had been starving for the Word, just like we had been. We would all go home from the men's study to questions from our wives. Questions about what we had studied, and what was next. It was like they were starving for anything we could share with them, eating of the crumbs from the table, but not actually being fed.

"We have to change this," we thought. We couldn't continue to starve our wives of this wonderful feast the Lord was providing. At the Followers church, women are basically second-class citizens. They're lesser than the men in everything. They eat after the men. They don't have a voice in the crowd, and they're expected to learn about Biblical things at home from their husbands, and that was final!

We were so tired of so many traditions at the church. So many we felt were just wrong and not what the Bible taught. How the women were being treated was a big one for all of us. We didn't agree with the church's stance on keeping them under our feet.

"Let's change things. Let's do a group Bible study with all of our wives and any other women who want to come too." We agreed and started our group study on Saturday nights. The men's study was 8am to noon (or sometimes longer), then we would come back with our wives at 6pm until midnight, most of the time.

Saturdays were amazing! When we started the men's study, we knew we were breaking the "unwritten" rules of the church, but now we were doing a study with the women. This was a big deal, and also a BIG no-no. We were able to keep the men's study relatively quiet and hidden from the church, but with a group study, we all knew that wouldn't be the case. It was going to get out, and we were going to feel the heat. Things were going to heat up for us all, little did we know how hot it would get.

The group study started much like the men's study did, with a lot of tears. The women had a lot of baggage that the men didn't. One of the struggles was stepping out of their old role that had them beneath us men, to their new place that had them beside us. For most of their lives the women had to eat after the men had taken what they wanted. Now, the men were saying, "Ladies first."

This transition has been hard for some of the women to get used to, especially at the Bible studies. Most of the women didn't say a word for the first few group studies, but after some prompting, they began to join in. Having their input was so valuable to the group. It wasn't long before all were in step with the study and each other. The Holy Spirit was leading us into the unknown, but He had us together.

The study went from ten people to twenty, then thirty. After a couple of months, forty people were there with us. The Lord was calling so many. It was like the early church in Acts 2:46-47: *"And day by day, attending the temple together and breaking bread in their homes, they received their food with glad and generous hearts, praising God and having favor with all the people. And the Lord added to their number day by day those who were being saved."*

The group was growing by leaps and bounds. Was this the beginning of a revival? We would hear a name on the horizon asking questions, and then before you knew it, they were at the study with us. We were at Brad's house, and it was getting tight. We'd move all the furniture out to the back porch and set up chairs four or five deep. Then there were fifty and then sixty people at the study. We had outgrown the house, and parking was getting to be an issue as well. Then we hit eighty people, and something had to be done.

I think it was Brad and Luke that found an old fire station with a big meeting area upstairs, very similar to a grange, that was available to rent. We formed a 501c3, rented the fire station, and officially started the Sunset Gospel Fellowship Bible Study. The Lord continued to bring people to us, the study quickly went from 80 people to 100, then 120 and topped out at about 150 people at its max.

It was a wonderful time being on this journey together. A few times a spy would come to the study to try and find something to report back to the church. We always knew who they were and why they were there. We'd hear crazy stories of what we were doing, how one of the women was dressed inappropriately or some other made-up lie. We knew we would be under spiritual attack even worse when we went public with the official study group. It happened, and it was ridiculous what people would make up, and even worse, what people would believe.

The group of men that started the studies were still at the core managing both studies. We would meet and vote on what would be the next study and discuss business needs of the new 501c3. We made some changes, and it started to look a little different from a typical Bible study. We would start the study with a couple of worship songs. Gary would most often lead the worship, with others filling in from time to time. Prayer ended up looking a little different, too. With nearly 150 people, the model of corporate prayer just wouldn't work. Prayer would sometimes last over an hour. So, we changed it. We went to taking prayer requests and only a couple people or even one person would be chosen to pray for the group. That seemed to work well, so we continued to use that model.

When the core would meet, these questions were starting to come up. "Are we becoming a church? Should we?" I think each of us had concerns about both questions, so we just continued on, praying the Lord would guide us into the future. One big change we made was to include people that had left the Followers church in the past, and even a bigger change was to include people that had never been a Follower at all. Both of these changes came with confrontation from within and from outside of our group. Remember, at Followers, if you leave the church, you are to be shunned and almost considered to be dead to those still at the church. Fellowshipping with those outside of the church was a huge deal that was met with anger from people still within the church, most of the time.

We felt drawn to open the study to everyone the Lord was bringing to us. We collectively knew God was doing things to grow us as new believers, and God seemed to be challenging us to drop the old baggage we were clinging to. We needed to look to Scripture and pray for guidance. It was hard, very hard at times, to let go of tradition, and to look forward to what God seemed to have before us. We'd been so conditioned to fear everything that we didn't understand. Fear it and shun it, was our first response, and this made change very, very difficult.

All that being said, we were still on fire for the Lord. These new ideas were scary, but so exhilarating at the same time.

25

◆

Together

By spring of 2018, a few of our group had started sneaking out and going to "real" church. Listening to their reports on how wonderful hearing a sermon in person was, had me so intrigued. At the Followers church if there was a holiday, like Memorial Day weekend or Christmas, church would be canceled. Also, if there was a funeral scheduled on a Sunday there wouldn't be a church service either.

One Sunday, there was a funeral planned. I thought, "This is my chance to go to 'real' church with my friends."

I asked my wife to come with me. She said, "Not a chance!" She thought it was too dangerous and had no interest. I went without her, driving out of town as fast as I could, hoping I wouldn't be seen. My heart was pounding with anticipation of the unknown. Would all the things I'd been fed about "worldly" churches be true? What if they were the fake, deceptive things we'd been taught they were? Truthfully, I didn't really know what to expect.

Finally, I turned the corner and saw the church and the sign out front. Good Shepherd Community Church. I liked the name and there were several guys in yellow safety vests helping me to find a parking spot. OK, that was unexpected, but I liked it. As I walked through the vast parking lot, there were more yellow vested men, joyfully greeting me with a "Good morning!" and "Right this way to the doors."

So far so good. I walked in and...WOW! I'd never seen anything like it. It was beautiful. There's a big school attached to the church building. The school hallway walls were painted with vast murals of animals and trees, and all kinds of beautiful scenes. I wandered around in awe. In the middle of the building complex was a large open area. In this space there were chairs and couches to relax in. Then to my surprise...a coffee shop! What? A coffee shop? It wasn't just a coffee cart, no, it was a Starbucks size coffee shop.

Looking back, I must have had my mouth wide open in surprise as I wandered in. The people serving coffee greeted me with a warm "Hello," and asked if I'd ever been there before? I said no, and they said, "Welcome! Your first coffee is free. Anything you want is on us."

"Really?" I asked.

"Yep!" they joyfully said. I didn't think I'd have time to finish the coffee before the church service started. They said it was OK to take the coffee in with me to the sanctuary. Again, my mind was blown! "Really? I can take it into the sanctuary?" This was all so new. They gave me my coffee and off I went.

I stood in the doorway to the sanctuary and marveled at the size of it. I didn't know how many people it would hold, but WOW, it was huge, it even had an upper area. I scanned the crowd and found my friends about four rows from the stage. I went down to them and sat in an aisle seat just in case it was too much for me and I had to leave.

I'd listened to hundreds of sermons before that day, but never in person. I was so nervous and excited at the same time. The lights dimmed and the worship team took the stage. I'd been secretly listening to modern worship music on the radio for a few years by then. Years before I had my eyes open to grace, I drove a dump truck at work. I spent a lot of time waiting to be called into the construction sites for my truck to be filled with dirt. As I waited, I would listen to the radio to pass the time. I didn't like talk radio, when the DJs would jabber on with mindless chatter. One day, I was pushing the buttons looking for a good song. The radio landed on a song that immediately had me hooked. I didn't know who was singing the song at the time, but I almost started to cry as I listened to the words. I didn't understand why I was so moved; the words didn't really make sense to me. The singer sang, *"I can only imagine when that day comes, and I find myself standing in the Son. I can only imagine."*

The song was so powerful to me, I wanted to hear it again, but didn't know who sang it. Sometime later, I found out the name of the band was MercyMe. It was a Christian band. I was scared to listen to a Christian radio station, especially when they talked about praying for people. I would turn to the station hoping to hear that song again, but then there would be another song that would catch my ear. One by one, starting with that MercyMe song, I started to really enjoy the music. I didn't understand what they were talking about most of the time, but I still enjoyed listening to them.

I knew a lot of old hymns and gospel songs, but strangely I didn't hear Jesus in these songs, I only thought about God the Father. My mind would always go to, "This song is about God." My faith that God was real was very strong from my youth, but it is so strange Jesus just didn't hit my radar until that day when the pastor came to our church with the message of grace.

Now back to the story. I was at Good Shepherd Church and the worship team was just taking the stage. They sang a couple of songs I recognized from the radio, and then they sang 'Amazing Grace/My Chains Are Gone.' I'd never heard this version before. The words of Amazing Grace broke me. *"How precious did that grace appear the hour I first believed!"*

I started to cry, and then this new version of the song changed, and the worship team sang, *"My chains are gone, I've been set free, My God, my Savior has ransomed me. And like a flood His mercy reigns. Unending love... Amazing Grace."*

At that moment my eyes locked with the eyes of the singer, and I broke down. I started to ugly cry. I sat down and sobbed. Jason, who was standing singing next to me, sat down and patted me on the back, asking if I was going to be OK. I said, "I don't think so!"

The pastor came out and preached on Joseph being tempted by Potiphar's wife. I soaked up every word. Hearing a sermon in person is so different than listening to one on the radio. I think it's so important being with the body of Christ at church, together, listening to a sermon being preached. It is so important, and I think that's what the Holy Spirit wants of us too. To be gathered together, worshiping our King and Savior.

I was on fire after the service! I thought, "That's it! I'm done with the Followers church! I'm going to Good Shepherd from now on!"

My wife said, "Are you crazy? No way! We need to stay and make changes here." At that time, she hoped we could be the ones to change the Followers' hearts—not God. All my hopes were dashed.

Our new life together as brothers and sisters in Christ was a gift from God. We were quickly losing friends and family out at Followers, due to us wanting to read the Bible, but it was even more than that. I think it was because the darkness hates the Light. We were now seeing what had been hidden from us our entire lives. Truth. When you live in a place that holds to tradition over truth, there's going to be conflict when you start to stand up for truth.

At that time, I wrote this little poem titled "Together" as a way to try and explain what we were going through that year. The storm was getting rough out at the church, and within our families as well. Try and picture each word, it will help you see what I'm trying to say.

Together

I was awakened by a crash.

All seemed wrong where I was.

My world was turned upside down as I felt the ship starting to list and sink.

When I reached the deck, I could see others unlashing a small boat from its place and start lowering it over the side.

A storm was raging.

A storm with such power it caused me to just stand and marvel at it for a time.

The waves were crashing over us.

The wind was blowing the rain sideways into our faces.

I looked around, and so many people we loved were just lying there on the deck not wanting us to wake them, fighting and kicking against us as we pleaded with them to join us.

The storm raged on.

It was so dark.

We had to go soon before all was lost.

As I joined them in the small boat, they called for me to hurry.

Someone yelled out "The ship is sinking!"

We had to push away or be destroyed.

Together we pushed away into the storm, leaving those we love behind.

Together we pulled on the oars,

Together into the darkness we went, clinging to one another, holding each other up as the storm raged,

We pulled together into the unknown, our feet being soaked by our tears.

The reflection of the ship burned on our faces, as we huddled tightly together.

Together we prayed.

Into the darkness we went, not knowing where to row, not knowing when the storm would subside.

Such a long night.

Our hands raw from the oars,

Our knees raw from the prayers.

And then in the distance came an orange glow,

A beam of light tearing through the darkness, guiding us to the dawn.

We could see our Savior in the light, holding that little boat on course towards Him.

Together towards the shore we went, with the memory of the ship sinking and the loved ones we left behind.

In the wind we could hear our Savior say, "keep our eyes on Him and not to the past."

Together we rowed, with our Savior guiding us towards the dawn, towards the shore and on to a life we could never imagine.
Oh Lord, thank you for guiding us, saving us and holding us...
Together.

Together was all we had. Life at the church was getting harder and harder. The Lord still had blinders on us, keeping our eyes on Him and not the coming storm.

26

Baptism

The year 2018 was a year of great growth and change. It was a year of joy and of sorrow, and it was also the year of baptisms.

If you read the Bible at all, baptism will come up, and come up it did. At the Followers church, baptisms had stopped when Walter, the last pastor, had died in 1969. Also at the Followers church, it was taught that if there was any chance to be saved and go to heaven, you had to be baptized by Walter or another "called man."

Well, this caused a problem for my generation. Walter died six months before I was born, and no one had been "called" to take his place. How was I going to be saved? I was told that I was saved by my grandfather's baptism. I've heard others in our group say that they were told the same type of thing, that they were saved by their parents or grandparents baptisms.

"Don't worry, God will make a way. Maybe God baptized you when you were in the shower or out in the rain," a few older men out at the church had told me. In my experience, if you asked the older men any questions about the traditions we held to and why, they would become hostile and try and belittle you in front of others to shut you up. So needless to say, baptism wasn't talked about very often in the circles I was around. But again, if you read the Bible at all, baptism will be something you'll have to take a hard look at. For us, this was true.

Baptism...I'd seen one on a TV show once and heard the word

before, but I really didn't know anything about what it was or why. Like I've written, all many of us knew about baptism, is that it was something from our past that we no longer did.

Some of the people in the Bible study group started to talk about baptism and began thinking it was something we needed to do. Others disagreed. Their argument was that we were saved by grace and not by our baptism, so we didn't need to do it, or hit that "beehive" causing us to get stung by the church. We were already in enough trouble out at the church for studying the Bible, why bring more anger on us?

We talked at great length about baptism and if we should do it. It even caused some division within our ranks. Marshall had worked with a pastor at his job and felt this pastor could help us with our concerns and disagreements. It was suggested we invite him to a BBQ at Jason's house and get to know him first, and then see if he would come to the Bible study and talk with us there about baptism.

Now, you need to understand how big of a deal both of these things were in our group. We were pushing the traditions and rules to their breaking points, and it was getting real. Doing a small men's Bible study could be overlooked by the church. A group Bible study was, for some at the church, too much and a cause for shunning us. Inviting people who had left the Followers church in the past to the Bible study, was so out of line, their heads were about to explode. But when we started to talk about baptism, that was the last straw!

If anyone knew we had invited a pastor to a BBQ at one of our homes, it would have been the end for us right then. So we had to be very careful to keep it quiet. Fear of losing it all still had its hooks in us.

The day of the BBQ came. Marshall introduced Pastor Aeric to me, and we chatted a little. He seemed like a good guy. He was actually the first pastor I'd ever really spoken to. I stayed back a little and just watched him in the crowd, trying to see his character, and if I could tell if he really was a good guy or not. He seemed to be genuine and someone who could be trusted.

The day went well, and we decided to ask Pastor Aeric to one of the next group Bible studies. He agreed, and if this were a movie, this is where the scene would pan to the horizon where a giant storm full of black clouds was looming, an angry looking storm, churning, full of lightning. A storm we couldn't see at the time, but a storm that was coming towards us faster than we could ever imagine.

The group study had been going for about six or seven months by this time. On any given Saturday night, the typical attendance was around 120 or more. We'd opened it to anyone who wanted to come, from our past and also from our future. We had endured many changes, highs and lows, within the group. We had close brothers and sisters turn their backs on us. But they weren't really turning their backs on us, they were turning their backs on Jesus. They were seeking to save their old lives it seems.

"For whoever would save his life will lose it, but whoever loses his life for my sake will find it." Matthew 16:25.

This scripture was used to shore up faith healing to us, but what we were experiencing at the time is the actual explanation, you must be willing to follow Jesus, no matter the cost.

God had drawn us together like a beautiful bouquet, tying us tightly together, so each flower could show the gifts the Lord had chosen for them and the season when they would bloom. But God has His will, and His will is for us to follow Him regardless of the cost. And no matter what you hear, following the Lord will cost you everything.

Pastor Aeric came to the study and quietly sat listening to everyone's ideas about baptism and if we needed it or not. After a long while of listening, Aeric said, "I hear all of your concerns about baptism, but what if the reason you got baptized was because Jesus said to? Wouldn't that be a good enough reason?" Aeric continued, "That's not the real reason you should, actually baptism means a lot more than just obedience, but let's just wipe the table clean with Jesus said we should, and that's a good enough reason."

The room went quiet. Our minds were reeling with this simple truth. Pastor Aeric then continued to teach us about what baptism really represented. We weren't saved by baptism. Baptism is an outward expression of an inward change. We looked through the Bible at many references, such as Acts 16:31-34: *"And they said, "Believe in the Lord Jesus, and you will be saved, you and your household." And they spoke the word of the Lord to him and to all who were in his house. And he took them the same hour of the night and washed their wounds; and he was baptized at once, he and all his family. Then he brought them up into his house and set food before them. And he rejoiced along with his entire household that he had believed in God."*

Jesus told us to believe in Him and be baptized. So, that's what we should do. In our time, as well as in the time of Jesus, being baptized might cost you your life. Planting your flag in Jesus' camp could get you killed in some countries or shunned from the only life you had ever known. In both cases you could lose your life, metaphorically speaking.

Was it worth the cost? Was it something we should do? Our group study quickly went from over 120 people to about sixty. The cost to give it all up for Jesus was just too high for some.

27

$\blacklozenge$

An Unsure Future

The baptisms were on the horizon it seemed, and with that, I had the feeling we would be kicked out of the church or be treated so poorly by friends and family we would want to leave. I was willing to leave the church as soon as I could. I'd spent a lifetime being treated, by most, like I didn't belong, and I was done with them. Good Shepherd, the church I had visited earlier that year, was still on my mind as a place I wanted to go to, but I had to convince my wife to give it a try.

My wife's family were very much Followers of the dead preacher Walter's traditions. Her grandfather was one of Walter's best friends. It was common to hear "Walter said this" or "Walter said that" at my in-laws house. My father-in-law has a very high opinion of his own intelligence. He thinks he's smarter than just about everyone around him, just ask him and he'll tell you. He had been trying to undermine me and our Bible study group from the first time he'd heard about us doing it. He tried to poison our kids against us, and other family members as well. His thoughts were that we were too ignorant to understand the Bible.

He also complained that if we wanted to know anything about the Bible, or needed spiritual leadership, why didn't we come to him? He told me he had read the Bible from cover-to-cover, and he also had heard Walter preach, so that gave him authority over me. But the worst thing he has said is that he's read the Bible, and it is full of errors. "It is a book written by men that were flawed, and because of that, the Bible is flawed and can't be trusted." He says that if he can't understand the Bible, how do we think we can?

My father-in-law also said we were just a bunch of dummies believing in this grace we kept talking about. He has even written a 60-page "manifesto" titled "Grace The Great Lie." In it, he called us at the Bible study "The Holy of Holies," and "Just a bunch of Bible thumpers."

He thought it would be an insult to call us that, but I see it as a compliment. What is the Holy of Holies? In the Old Testament, it's the inner sanctum of the temple, where God dwells. So my father-in-law's intended insult is actually correct—God DOES dwell inside us. But my father-in-law doesn't seem to understand that we are now the temple after what Jesus did on the cross, and the giving of the Holy Spirit to believers. *"Do you not know that you are God's temple and that God's Spirit dwells in you? If anyone destroys God's temple, God will destroy him. For God's temple is holy, and you are that temple." 1 Corinthians 3:16-17*

My heart breaks for him thinking that grace is a great lie. How could he say that? When I read about the stiff-necked Pharisees in the Bible, I see his face, I hear his words. His pride that he's so right because he thinks he knows better. The aggressive way he will fight against all reason, has made him a very, very difficult person to interact with.

My in-laws had been trying to meddle in and/or control my house since my wife and I were first married. Sadly, my wife was very susceptible to their control. They have caused so many problems in our marriage over the years, and it's not what the Bible teaches us to do.

Needless to say, my wife had an uphill battle before her. She had been so steeped in the idea that the Followers church was the "one right church," and that it had always been right, until things started to change after Walter died. All this had become an idol and getting her to even consider visiting another church was very difficult.

My wife had reluctantly listened to a few sermons here and there, most of the time with a very cynical approach. God had her on her own journey of discovery that at times caused conflict in our home, as well as with some of the other men in the group.

But God... He works His plan in mysterious ways. I introduced my wife to a pastor named Alistair Begg, and she was hooked. He has a strong Scottish accent and was enjoyable to listen to. I was so glad that my wife had found her footing. We Googled Alistair and found out his church was back in Ohio, and that he had a live stream on Sunday mornings at 6AM, our time. This was great! "Let's try live streaming his church and see what real church looks like."

My wife agreed (!) and we started doing this every Sunday morning. It was so good, for not only my wife to see, but for me as well. For my wife, this was the first "real" church she'd ever seen and, yes, real church is very different than cult church. She could see what we'd been talking about with worship music, and really, how a church service is conducted. I think most churches have a similar program.

I would drop a hint, that I would love it if she would go to Good

Shepherd with me some time. Most of the time she seemed to just ignore my prompting, and other times I was met with a strong push back that "she wasn't interested." God was being very patient with her, and I was trying to be as well.

Finally, after months of asking, she agreed to go and see what everyone had been talking about. I was so excited that she said yes! Sunday came and we headed out. I had worship music on, and we were singing along, it was so much fun. When we got to Good Shepherd, I couldn't wait to show her around. "Look at the beautiful murals! Do you want a coffee?" I was trying so hard to sell it.

A group of our friends were there for the service as well and this helped to ease my wife's mind. It was finally time for the service to start and we headed in. She thought the sanctuary was "just OK."

"Hmm...she seems to be looking for things to NOT like," I thought. "Wait until the worship team starts to sing, that will show her how great this place is."

The team came out, and it was...well... less than I had hoped for. I think maybe this was the team that was just learning how to sing and play their instruments. It was not good at all.

"OK... when the pastor gives his message it will be all she needs to be hooked like I was," I thought. Nope...they were just finishing up on one study and hadn't started the next one. That day was a very light service, focusing mainly on church business and upcoming events. Ugh! She wasn't impressed at all! "It's a nice place," she said, but she was not interested in ever going back.

I felt gutted. This was my only hope at the time, but again, God can be seen in my story here as well. Evidently, God didn't want what I thought I wanted. He had other plans for us.

The talk of some in our group about getting baptized was progressing from being a thought to a reality. My wife was so angry at the group. "Don't they know this will ruin everything?" she said. The word had gotten out that some were thinking about getting baptized and that's when that storm with the black cloud struck. People freaked out, and that's putting it mildly.

"WHO DO YOU THINK YOU ARE?" we'd be confronted with. My father-in-law was one who really freaked out on us. No exaggeration, I think he yelled at my wife for three days, in person and over the phone.

Now, just so you know, my wife is incredibly intelligent, and not one to back down from a fight. Sometimes that's good, sometimes not so much, but this time it was a really good quality for her to have in her character. When the possibility of our group getting baptized was more of a reality, she dove into the Bible for answers. God seemed to lead her down a path that she needed. A path to find the truth that would set it right in her head and heart. After days of study, she went from "I'll never" to "I understand now why" and she wanted to join them at the river.

This was just before her dad had come unglued, and thank You Lord! God gave her the armor to put on, just before she was attacked by her dad. All his ranting about "how dare we even think about baptism" and "that bell can't be un-rung" garbage, and then him getting in her face in a very heated confrontation. We were lucky our sons were there to defend her against his rage. This broke my wife's heart, that her dad would act that way against her, not wanting to even talk about it without screaming at her. My wife's the youngest child in her family and had always been a daddy's girl.

God was ripping at the fabric of her life, just like in Luke 12:53: *"They will be divided, father against son and son against father, mother against daughter and daughter against mother, mother-in-law against her daughter-in-law and daughter-in-law against mother-in-law."*

This revival that God had us in had us living out so many passages that we would read about in the Bible, and this was no exception. My wife was "all in" now and ready to go to the river, but she'd been very sick. She'd had pneumonia a few months before, and getting in the river to be baptized on a fall day might just kill her. I said, "I'm sorry, but you're not doing it this time. This is only the beginning, there will be more baptisms."

28

Oh Happy Day!

It was Friday night, and the baptisms were planned for the next day. The word had gotten out to everyone at Followers what we were doing, and we all knew the end of our time there was near. We gathered together that Friday evening at one of our houses. You could feel the electricity in the air, of excitement and of fear of the unknown. The excited conversations slowly turned to the reality that we were going to probably lose everything in the life we had known. We were going to give it all up to follow Jesus and we were ready to do so. We felt the weight of losing our families and friends. Some would lose a wife or a husband. Many would lose their children and grandchildren. For some it might be a job or their home. All to follow Jesus.

But God…He again was so gracious to us. He had gathered us together to follow him no matter the cost, but we weren't alone. We had each other, brothers and sisters in Christ. And most of all, we had the Lord. Before we went home, we gathered together and prayed, thanking the Lord for allowing us to be one of His, and for guiding us through the next chapter in His story.

Remember, this isn't my story or our story. No, this is God's story I'm writing about. From the first pages of my existence, God knew every page that would be written. Every blow I received; God knew. Every tear I cried; God knew. And everyone I would lose; God knew. It's God's story, because it all points to His Glory. The Light is so much brighter because of the darkness. His Glory is that much sweeter and more fragrant because of it.

We prayed a prayer of hope, a prayer for guidance, and a prayer of thanks for all the Lord had done in our lives.

Saturday was finally here, and we all went to the Willamette River. My wife and I weren't getting baptized that day, but we were so nervous nevertheless as we walked down the trail. I wondered if anyone we knew would be there to try and stop us or just stand off and mock us. I would never in my wildest dreams have imagined what was waiting for us down by the river.

People… lots and lots of people we didn't know. I don't know the count; I've heard there were close to 100 people at the river that day. Some say less, but all I know is, there were a lot of people waiting for us. There were even people we didn't know out in boats, cheering us on. We'd never seen the body of Christ before. It was so amazing.

Pastor Aeric had made it known that we were giving everything up to follow Jesus. The word had spread, and all these people were there to support us. We sang a couple of hymns: 'Amazing Grace,' 'Shall We Gather At The River,' and 'Oh, Happy Day.' The ones who were getting baptized gave their testimonies. This was very new to me, and I loved it.

After each baptism we clapped and cheered, the joy flooding over us and out of us. People in boats were cheering as they passed by, and fishermen on the far banks were cheering as well. It was a beautiful moment to be a part of, and it seemed like God's glory was washing over all who witnessed it.

Thirteen of our group were baptized that day. It was so amazing that we did it again the very next weekend, this time at the Milk Creek in Mulino. Thirteen more pledged their allegiance to King Jesus! God sure had us on fire for Him. What a glorious couple of days.

After these baptisms, we all sensed the anger... I want to say hate, at Followers. If not a hate, then a very deep dislike for our group, from the church and our families and friends. Several of our group had decided they were done going to Followers, and our numbers were slowly getting smaller at the church on Thursdays and Sunday.

I think the smaller our group got at church, the bolder the Followers got at verbally attacking us. My wife was adamant that we needed to stay at Followers and would confront the group saying, "We need to stay and fight to make a change out here."

The month of November 2018, the Lord started drawing our group away even faster. At the Followers church our group sat in the same area. After just a few weeks it was just my wife and I, sitting out there by ourselves. Then I didn't want to go on Thursday nights either. It was hard to be the only one from our group to stand on the back porch of the church before a service and be hated by 1,000 or so men. So, I have to say, my wife was the bravest of us all to continue going after the rest of us had decided to leave.

Then my wife had a change of mind and of heart. While praying for our group to stay and fight, the Lord opened her eyes that, "It is not your fight." She was now convinced that it wasn't for her to make the changes out at the Follower church. This was for God to do. Only He could open the eyes of the blind. Only God can change that whitewashed tomb.

One minute my wife was standing strong ready to fight for all she knew, and then just like a snap, she was changed and ready to consider something else. She came to me with an idea. She said that she'd been looking deeply into the church Pastor Aeric went to: New Life Church. She had seen on their website that they were considering a 9am service, and she was thinking about us going and seeing what they had to offer. I was so excited! I was so ready to follow my brothers and sisters to the new horizon. My wife said we could go to Pastor Aeric's church at 9am and still make it out to the Followers church, and no one would know.

Hmm…ok, it wasn't the break I'd hoped for, but it was a start. We drove to New Life Church and to my surprise, I recognized some of the people walking up the sidewalk. "Hey! I know those people," I thought. My brothers and sisters were coming to the service, too. I hadn't been in the loop that many were giving it a try. When the head pastor, Pastor Scott, came out of his office, there were about forty of us standing in the vestibule.

Pastor Scott had been wanting to try a 9am service, but didn't know why. He'd been talking with the elders of his church trying to convince them it was something they needed to do. It sounded like after much debate they agreed, never imagining there would be a group of lost sheep who desperately needed an earthly shepherd showing up that day.

Pastor Scott was preaching in the book of Romans. I'd never read Romans before, and my mind was blown. I looked around at my brothers and sisters as we all were soaking up every word Pastor Scott spoke. I noticed almost every cheek was wet with tears. What an experience! God is so good!

After the service, my wife and I were again on fire for the Lord, and so excited with our lights burning bright. We went directly to the Followers church and YUCK! It felt like death was all around us. It felt so dark and so dead. No joy like we'd just experienced. No hope... no Jesus.

My wife, full of joy, went to her sister with the news of what we'd just experienced, thinking she would be just as excited. We had thought she was on the same path as we were, just behind us a little, but still on the path. We were so very wrong! My wife gave her the news and her sister freaked out. "You had better tell Dad, or I will!" she said.

This gutted my wife and filled her with sorrow. She had hoped for more. Her sister didn't even want to speak to her anymore. They had an interaction a week or so later where her sister didn't want to be seen with my wife out at the church after a funeral. It was the end of their sisterhood, but we still pray that she will have her eyes opened to truth just like we have. We pray for all the ones that, just like in the poem I wrote, "were kicking against us, not wanting us to wake them."

Thanksgiving was near and we went to my in-laws for dinner. We were only there a short time, until my wife caught her dad talking badly about us to family in the other room. He was trying to undermine everything we believed in. There were angry words spoken, and then we left and went home. I think that was the last time I spoke to my wife's family. Just a couple of weeks later my wife got the call from her mom that we weren't welcome anymore. I got the call from Dan, and he said basically the same thing. If we were going to visit other churches and support the baptisms, we weren't welcome in the family anymore…We were shunned.

In a short amount of time, the shunning reached all of us. We were in the first group God harvested from the Followers church. There were about sixty of us in that first wave. God had decided it was time for us to move on and follow Him.

Most of our group landed in New Life Church where Pastor Scott and Aeric preached. Some found other churches that God was drawing them to. At first it seemed weird that we all didn't land in the same church, but after we realized that God was scattering us throughout the valley, it felt wonderful being attached to so many different churches.

I see the same thing in Acts 8 when the believers were scattered throughout the region. God scattered us too, and we were all telling our story of redemption and how grace had saved us from a dark place. It was wonderful how God used us to link so many churches in a really large area. Eventually my wife and I landed at a church about an hour's drive South. There will be about seventeen churches total we all land in, later in the story.

We had one more river baptism in December in the Clackamas River. Several more were baptized that day as well. We built a huge fire, so those who were getting baptized wouldn't freeze to death getting out of the cold river. What a wonderful day!

It's amazing to me how God sends out His believers through revival and through persecution, not only in Biblical times, but in our day as well.

29

A Gift From Thailand

God had another surprise for us: Pastor Tim and his wife Debbi.
Pastor Tim had spent years in Thailand shepherding a large group
of international workers. For reasons unknown to Tim at the time,
his contract there was ended, and he and Debbi were sent back
to the U.S. They were originally from California and Pastor Tim
thought that's probably where they would end up.

Instead, they ended up in the Pacific Northwest living near one of
their daughters while Pastor Tim looked for a church that needed
his services. Little did he know why God had drawn him to Oregon.
Little did he know how much God had for him to do.

Pastor Tim is, in my opinion, a true shepherd of God. He loves
God's sheep and works very hard to shepherd them well. His wife
Debbi is the sister everyone would want to have, and I would
imagine she's very similar to Phoebe in the Bible in her devotion to
serving God's people. Debbi loves everyone with the love of Jesus
and has also been so very needed in our lives.

Little did they know what a huge impact they both would have
when Pastor Tim took the job of Associate Pastor at New Life
Church. Pastor Tim had the job for only a year when about forty
lost, raggedy sheep showed up in the vestibule of New Life Church,
on that Sunday when we all first visited. I bet we were a sight to see.
I picture us as a little flock of sheep that had been out in the wilder-
ness our entire lives; our wool full of stickers and leaves, standing

there like those sheep from my youth, waiting to be looked after and cared for by an earthy shepherd.

Throughout my story there are moments where I feel you can see God working. God knew what we needed. God knew WHO we needed, and he was in Thailand. Can you look back over your life and see God in those moments you thought somehow you'd failed? Can you see him working through hard times that caused you to change the direction of your life, only to end up for the better? Well, I think this might be the case with Tim and Debbi. Pastor Tim made it a point to talk with each of us in depth, really getting to know who we were and what our needs were.

In the 23rd Psalm it says, *"Thy rod and Thy staff they comfort me."* I used to read this as under the shepherd's rod and staff I was protected, comforted, and safe. This is true… but let's look at what those shepherds' tools were actually used for.

The rod is typically a short, thick stick about two feet long. It could be used as a weapon to protect not only the shepherd, but also the sheep. But the main use for a rod is that it's a tool the shepherd would use to inspect the sheep's health. The shepherd would run it through the sheep's wool to inspect them for sickness or wounds. A sick or damaged sheep is hard to see at first glance. The rod allowed the shepherd to really take the time to inspect the sheep, beneath the outer wool that might be hiding things that could cause the sheep to fall to the wolves or die from unseen causes. Ezekiel 20:37 says *"I will make you pass under the rod, and I will bring you into the bond of the covenant."* The Lord uses the rod in Ezekiel as a word picture of how He, out of love for His sheep, brings us into His flock, looks over us and cares for us, and through His covenant with us, will never let us go.

Thy rod and Thy staff... The Shepherd would put his staff across the door to the sheepfold, only allowing one sheep at a time to pass, he would pass the rod over the sheep to inspect it and also count it as one of his.

The staff was a tool as well. When you think of what a shepherd looks like, you will most likely think of a person with a hooked staff. The hook on the staff would be used to grab a sheep from a distance. The Shepherd could gently hook the sheep and pull it closer to him so he could care for it.

The way Pastor Tim figuratively used all the tools of a shepherd was so needed to us sheep. I can see how the rod and staff comforted us. Just like an earthly shepherd, Pastor Tim looked over our spiritual health and tended to our broken hearts.

The gospel of John talks about how The Good Shepherd, Jesus, loves and takes care of His sheep. Pastor Tim has studied John 10 and is faithful in applying it. As one of those lost sheep needing an earthly shepherd to care for me, I'm sure glad he did.

It was now early December 2018 and there were so many things to learn about being a new Christian. Our first Advent season was so strange. I'd never heard of Advent before. What was this all about? People raising their hands during worship music? What are they doing? Did we make a mistake, and this was a strange church?

We had so much baggage. And then there was Communion. Oh man... "Isn't that a Catholic tradition?" my wife and I asked each other.

At times I didn't know what to do or think. We would talk about all the new things we were experiencing with the group, and it wasn't just New Life Church doing these things. It seemed all the churches were doing Advent, Communion, and other things too. All the things we were now doing we'd been taught against at Followers Church or were totally new to us. This was so good for us to know, and we needed Pastor Tim and his wife Debbi to walk beside us through it all, helping us to navigate and explain the truth.

During this time of growth, it seemed we were a lot like the lead character, Christian, in John Bunyan's allegory *The Pilgrim's Progress*. We were saved just like Christian was, at the Wicket Gate, when we received Jesus Christ as our Savior and King. But just like Christian, we carried a burden that we didn't need to. We all had this burden or what I call "baggage." We needed help to understand that we could drop it all at the foot of the Cross. Just like Christian in the allegory, we carried our burdens for far too long.

Very shortly after joining New Life Church, my wife and I were asked to join a life group, or what some may call a home group study. Pastor Tim and his wife Debbi; Dale, who was an elder in the church, and his wife Cris; Marshall and his wife Jennifer; Mark and his wife Amy; and a young widow, Kimberly (who was also from Followers) were our new little family we would meet with every week. We would eat dinner together and then discuss questions about the Sunday sermon. Being in a life group was exactly what we needed. We needed to have a place, and a group of people, that quickly became so very close to us. A safe place to learn, to cry, to grow, and to heal.

We had never heard of a life group before coming to New Life

Church. If you ever have a chance to join one, I strongly recommend it. Just like being baptized, we were being completely submerged in this new life as Christians, learning to die to ourselves, and being raised back up, by all of these wonderful mature Christians and pastors the Lord was surrounding us with.

The Lord knew we needed these shepherds so badly. Thank you Lord, for giving them the patience to deal with our brokenness. Thank you Lord, for giving them the truth they spoke into our lives.

Thank you Lord, for the love of a shepherd like Pastor Tim, and his wife Debbi.

30

◆

Our Turn

After the New Year, my wife and I heard there were going to be more baptisms coming up, but this time they were going be inside at New Life Church in their baptistery tank. We talked it over and decided we wanted to get baptized this time.

The day of the baptisms came, February 17, 2019, and New Life Church was filled to the brim with people. God had knitted our group into so many churches. It was amazing how the body of Christ could gather together and rejoice in our baptisms.

Before we gave our testimonies, we sang a couple of worship songs. The singing was so powerful, I think it shook the dust off the rafters. We were told by many of the older, long-time members of New Life Church that it was one of the most powerful days they'd witnessed. We had so much joy and our emotions were raw. There are memories in your life that you never want to forget. For me, this was one of those moments. We'd been freed from the chains of darkness just a couple of months before, and the Light appeared so much brighter because of the darkness. The Light seemed to be infectious to all the churches that God had put us in.

We've been told that our group, through the working of the Holy Spirit, has brought a renewed fire to so many. What a wonderful thing to be a part of. To see the joy and fellowship in all these new people we didn't know before. In Matthew 19:29 it says, *"And every-one who has left houses or brothers or sisters or father or mother or children or lands, for My name's sake, will receive a hundredfold and will inherit eternal life."*

We found this to be so true. We'd given up all these things. But God was again true to His word in the gifts spoken about in Matthew 19. God gave us "a hundredfold" of people who we love and who love us. I found it strange at first that I could deeply care for—no, deeply love—people I'd only known for a short time. I really think it's because of the Holy Spirit that is inside of us. When you meet a fellow Christian, don't you feel a connection? It's really odd, right? I think it's because our spirit is the same Holy Spirit. The Spirit is drawing us together, binding us to one another, molding us into the body of Christ. At any of our gatherings, it wouldn't be unusual to have many different pastors from different churches in the crowd.

We were still "firehose learning" in what it looked like to be a Christian. Pastor Tim started an Adult Bible Class (ABC) and we studied the Gospel of Mark. It was so amazing to study the Bible under a pastor's teaching. We'd never had Sunday school at the Followers church. I felt like I needed to sit in the little kids' class and learn the basics with them. It was wonderful to be able to attend an Adult Bible Class. The Bible came alive each week.

Pastor Tim took a few of us men from the group and called us his "Bereans." He started a text group so he could speak into our lives almost every day. He would pass on Scripture that he wanted us to read and then give our feedback on it. He would also challenge us to do what the Bereans did in the Bible, to look to Scripture every day to see if what he was telling us was true and accurate. Over time,

Pastor Tim had the "Bereans" write a sermon and have him review and grade it, then give a chapel service to a retirement community in the area. Pastor Tim also challenged us to write and teach studies on different chapters in 1st and 2nd Samuel. We would record the studies on an audio file that was then downloaded to New Life's web page (if you're interested in listening to them).

Easter was approaching, as well as Good Friday. Out at the Followers church, Easter was all about rabbits and dressing in your best. You'd typically have a fancy dinner with family. I knew there was some Biblical reason why we celebrated Easter, but I didn't really think about it much. The Saturday before Easter Sunday, the Followers have a big Easter egg hunt. It's a big deal and comes with a carnival-like atmosphere. Teenage girls dress up like rabbits and hand out candy. There's a raffle to win a bunny rabbit, too. Rabbits, candy, and balloons, but no Jesus. We didn't know about Jesus and the Cross, so why would we understand what Easter really represents. Good Friday, if I'd ever heard about it, sounded like a Catholic church tradition. Oh, how wrong we were!

Our first Good Friday service at New Life Church left us without words. To come to an understanding of what happened at the Cross and why, wrecked us. We were all in tears. It was so moving, and wonderful at the same time, it was almost hard to process the emotions simultaneously.

"It's Friday, but Sunday's coming!" I pray Good Friday and Easter services never lose their power in my life or in yours. Resurrection Sunday is my favorite Sunday of the year! What a blessing to have had our eyes open to truth.

There were so many fantastic and moving things we were now doing, but the spiritual warfare continued to attack us. Everything wasn't all roses and rainbows. For me, I had so many times where I felt like I couldn't keep up with the rest of the guys in their understanding of scripture. It left me feeling less or dumb that I sometimes struggled to grasp it all as quickly as they did. Old baggage with new experiences, coupled with a lack of understanding of the process, caused misunderstandings that led to hurtful conversations from some of the ones I looked up to. I felt like I was studying more and more to try and keep up with my brothers and Pastor Tim, rather than to know the Lord better. Seasoned Christians can tend to think everyone is where they are in their walk with the Lord. For me, being laughed at or mocked or even berated because I don't know all the ins and outs of being a Christian is very hard. The "tough love" approach can be very discouraging, at least it was for me. It seemed like for a time, I couldn't get anything right. I was definitely still on milk and not ready for the meat (or the mallet.)

God wasn't finished working out at the Followers church. We might have been the first wave to leave Followers, but God was already working on the hearts of a second wave that the Holy Spirit was calling to the Lord. It's interesting that many of those God was calling to, were the same ones that gave our group a lot of grief when we were coming to Christ the year before. I thought it interesting when they would tell us, "You guys did it wrong, and we're going to do it right."

In their opinion, when we did our Bible study, we somehow did it wrong. Also, when and how we left Followers, we did wrong as well.

I never heard why we did it wrong, but evidently in their eyes we did. The funny thing is, the second wave of people that would come out, started their own Bible study thinking they could "do it right," refusing to ever visit our study. They ended up doing very similar things that we had done, but on a much smaller scale. The third wave criticized them in similar ways, as they did to us, and so on. It's probably human nature to think we're better or have it figured out. I think it was probably spiritual warfare trying to keep us apart as well. United we are stronger and that's what the evil ones fear.

Eventually both Bible studies came to an end. God had used both studies as a lifeboat, in a way, to gather us together and get from the sinking ship to the shore. His purpose had been achieved and we were scattered into good churches, learning from good pastors, and getting plugged into the programs in each of these churches.

How many people are we talking about, you might ask? I don't know the exact number, but I've heard up to 350 people have had their eyes open to grace. That's amazing! Out of a group of about 2,000 people out at the Followers church, to have that many people in such a short time have their eyes opened! Only God has the power to do that!

Regardless when or how you came to Jesus, we all need to remember this… With every prayer we pray, we need to remember what the Lord has done for us and cry out, "Thank you Lord! Oh thank you Lord!"

With every new day we get to live in His grace, we need to cry out, "Thank you Lord, oh, thank you Lord!"

And as we bend our knee before Him when He calls us home, we need to cry out, "Thank you Lord…oh thank you Lord!"

Without the Lord and His amazing grace, this story wouldn't have ever happened. I would've probably died a sad statistic, forgotten to time.

But God…

31

◆

More Chapters Still to Write

God seemed to have a new chapter in our lives to write. He's taken us out of our comfort zone and moved us into the unknown.

After a couple of years at New Life Church, God moved my wife and me to a new church about an hour south of everyone and everything we had ever known. We now attend Emmanuel Bible Church. We still stay in touch with our brothers and sisters from the Bible study, but not as often as before. It was hard leaving the comfort of our friends and the solid Bible teaching of New Life Church, but again, it was like we could do nothing but follow the Lord's calling. When God moved us to Emmanuel Bible Church it was really hard at first. The spiritual warfare hit us and our family hard.

We eventually got plugged in, but it was like we needed to be re-potted so we could grow. The first time I walked into Emmanuel Bible Church, I felt like I'd taken a drink of water and didn't know how thirsty I really was. It's interesting how God uses different things to move you in the direction He wants you to go. A little nudge here, or a kick there. We are sheep, and sometimes need a poke from the Shepherd's goad to get us moving. I found my footing and realized it was OK that I didn't know as much as everyone around me. I didn't feel like I was failing anymore. I needed to be re-potted. It's been so good for both my wife and me.

We didn't realize how much we were being affected by the Followers in the area we had just moved from. For some in our group, running into someone you love at the store or at a restaurant, and being shunned doesn't bug them that badly. But for some, especially my wife, it was almost more than she could bear. It took us months in our new home to not walk into a store and have the stressful look-around to see who we might know and want to avoid. We felt so free from it. Even now, when we drive back up to visit friends near where we used to live, it comes with a heaviness and trepidation. I hope that will someday pass.

The new chapters in our life that God is writing have us on so many new adventures. My wife and I visited Israel on a vacation, and it was wonderful to see the places we'd only read about in the Bible. I see the world in pictures and tend to speak that way too, so actually seeing where Jesus walked, it all now comes alive in my Bible studies. Recently, Pastor Tim, Debbi, Mark, Amy, my wife and I got the opportunity to go to Greece and walk in the footsteps of the apostle Paul, visiting Corinth, Athens, Philippi, Thessalonica and Berea. What an amazing experience we got to have with people we love so dear.

Both my wife and I have been blessed to experience men's and women's retreats. We've also had many ministry opportunities to serve in the church. I feel like I've grown in ways I couldn't have imagined. We joined a two-year program called ELLS (Equipping Leaders for a Lifetime of Service.) It was great! I was really drawn to this program, as well as the second most influential earthly shepherd I'd ever had: Pastor Stan.

He and Pastor Tim are so very similar in their ability to be, what I see, the epitome of what an earthly shepherd of God's sheep should be like. Pastor Stan, just as Pastor Tim had done, came alongside my wife and I and spoke into our lives. After his sermons, we feel like we've really been fed. He challenges us to dive deeper into the Word, as well as diving deeper into love with our Savior, Jesus Christ.

The ELLS class was so amazing to take. I think I need to go through it again, there's so much to learn. Pastor Stan took the time to get to know me and asked if we could meet every week for almost a year to talk through the PTSD from my childhood. I didn't know that he was a trained counselor as well. I was able, after fifty years, to finally be at peace with the horrors I told you about at the beginning of this book. I still have the memories, but the sting of it all is now gone. I think God allowed me to go through those dark times so I can speak to abuse and redemption from experience. I can help someone who's been abused in a way someone who hasn't, just wouldn't understand. We've also had the opportunity to talk with others who have come out of cults in the area, about the baggage they might have and how we were able to overcome traditions with truth.

After I completed the ELLS program, Pastor Stan asked if I would go with him and a team to Kenya, Africa. ELLS teaches the rural pastors in Kenya, and other African countries, how to rightly divide the Scriptures and how to build a sermon and teach it correctly. I feel so fortunate that I had the opportunity to go. It was really interesting and wonderful to be a part of this ministry. I gave my testimony about what the Lord has done in my life at each of the trainings we did. The team ended up teaching about 1,000 pastors and Sunday school teachers from all over Kenya and surrounding countries. You don't have to be a pastor or elder to have Acts 20:24

as a life verse. *"But I do not account my life of any value nor as precious to myself, if only I may finish my course and the ministry that I received from the Lord Jesus, to testify to the gospel of the grace of God."*

God is so good! It seems like this is what the Lord wants of me in this chapter of my life, to tell God's story to whoever will listen. I've had the opportunity to tell God's story, that I've been blessed to be a part of, to so many people at home as well as overseas. I would have never thought I would go on a mission trip, let alone stand in front of hundreds of people, not only in Africa, but here at home as well, and share the Lord with them. In my old life, it just never would have happened. In my old nature, I would've gotten too nervous to speak in front of a crowd, but now, it doesn't make me nervous at all to tell God's story. I'm so excited to see what the Lord has for me next! I only hope that I can do it well and bring Him glory.

If you're wondering what's happened to the "Bouquet of Brothers" who the Lord called to grace at the beginning of the revival, I think we all are in some sort of ministry with the churches where we've landed. Some are elders of their churches, some are Sunday School teachers, some are worship team leaders, some are evangelists, and I believe we're all small group leaders as well.

I think it's interesting that God chose this small group of men to start a revival in a dark place. We weren't looking for Jesus when He showed up. We had no idea what we were doing most of the time. But God didn't care. He only asked us to believe in Him and follow His call.

Are you hearing God's call? Are you willing to follow Him regardless of the cost?

Thank you Lord for my life. The dark days and the Light. The hard times and the good. It's Your story, Lord. I hope I've told it well, bringing You the glory in it all.

I remembered back to what my mom told me before she died. I remember she said to me that the most important thing I needed to know about her was that she was a Christian. I look back at that and it brings me so much joy and peace!

Yes! Thank you Mom, I get it now. I understand what you were saying to me all those years ago. You were a Christian, and now so am I!

Thank you reader for being with me on this journey. I'm so glad you were. Thank you for not leaving me there alone in those hard pages to read.

I hope you've enjoyed the journey. And remember, the most important thing you need to know about me is…I'm a Christian.

Epilogue

◆

In the process of finishing this book, my little sister sadly passed away. It seems she had been ill for a while and didn't seek medical attention due to still being at the Follower church. She had a stroke and passed away at only 50 years old. I didn't go to her funeral because I knew I wouldn't be welcome, but sent flowers and my love. I'm sorry sis, I wish things could have been different between us.

God is so interesting! About a year before my sister's death, my dad called my desk phone at work. He had done this before in the past, always leaving a very aggressive message that said, "This is your father, call me!"

This time when he called, his tone seemed to be different. This time the message was, "Hi, this is your dad, could you call me if you have a chance? I would love to talk with you."

I decided to call him this time because his manner seemed so changed, and his conversation was too. He told me he had been very sick. He was now on oxygen with a pacemaker and was confined to a wheelchair. We had a short, but good, conversation. He asked about my wife and kids, something he'd never done before. I was at work so I couldn't talk long, but after we hung up, I truthfully hoped he would die before we had another conversation and ruined the only pleasant conversation we'd ever had.

A year went by with only one other very short and odd conversation with him, several months before my sister's death. After I found out my little sister had died, I called my dad to let him know she had passed. I knew no one else would. She was his daughter, and I felt he needed to know. He was surprised and saddened to hear the news and thanked me for the call.

When my sister died, I prayed that God would use her death to shine His light into a dark place and to use her death to bring Him glory. At the time, I was thinking about my sister's husband and her kids, hoping they would come to know the Lord.

At work when a family member dies, we get three days off with pay. On the day of my sister's funeral, my middle son had the day off too. He asked me if I wanted to spend the day with him due to us not being welcome at the funeral. I said that would be wonderful. God has blessed my wife and me with all three of our sons and their wives becoming believers in Jesus Christ as their Savior and walking this journey with us. Thank you Lord!

My son and I had a great day together. We had a really good, deep conversation when my son told me he had been feeling a strong urge to contact my dad. We talked about it, and I gave him my dad's number.

A few days later my son called me to tell me about his conversation with my dad. He told me that my dad had been very ill and encouraged me to visit him soon. He then said something that took me by surprise. He said, "Dad, I think your dad might be a believer..." He told me about their conversation and honestly, I didn't know how to process it. The horrible abusive man you've been reading about in this book was now a believer in Christ?

I didn't really want my dad back in my life. He'd always made a mess of my life, and of me. I also didn't want to let my son down by not giving my dad a chance. I was dragging my feet and just not wanting to think about it, maybe even hoping my dad would pass before I had the chance to see him, and thus giving me an excuse.

A couple of weeks went by, and when my wife and I were out of town with friends, my son texted me with the news my dad had gotten worse and was now in the hospital and it didn't look good. He was really sick and might not make it much longer. I thought, "Maybe I'll visit him in a couple days after I return home, if he's still alive..."

We headed home the next day and dropped our friends off at their house. We live about an hour south of them and we started our drive home. I was thinking I would visit my dad tomorrow when I'm nearer the hospital. When we were about fifteen minutes away from home, our oldest son called us. We answered and he told us that he had visited my dad in the hospital. This was a surprise to me, because our oldest son had never had a connection with my dad.

He said, "I visited your dad today, and... I think he's a believer."

I pulled the car over and parked it. I said, "Say that again."

He said, "I think your dad's a believer!"

He then gave us his account of their conversation. His story was so compelling that my wife and I decided to turn the car around and drive the hour to see my dad for ourselves. When we walked in, my dad was very surprised to see us. He looked old and thin, and I could tell he'd been sick for a long time, and I doubted he would last much longer.

We had a good conversation. It wasn't the typical conversation we'd had in the past. He told me how he and his new wife had found a church that they had been going to, and how the congregation loves and prays for him. How they had been supporting him and his wife during this time of him being so sick.

I asked him. "Dad, is Jesus Christ your Savior?"

He said without hesitation, "ABSOLUTELY HE IS!" This made me very happy to hear. It almost took my breath away. Visitation time was ending, and we had to go. He asked if I would please visit him again, and I said I would and shook his hand. My mind was spinning on the drive home.

Two days later I visited him again during my lunch hour. It was just him and me this time. We had a good conversation…it felt a little guarded, but it was still good in an odd way. Before I left, I asked my dad if I could pray with him. He said, "Please! Yes," as he held up his hands towards me. As I took his hands and prepared myself to pray, I had to take a moment. I was holding the hands that had beat me so many times. I was holding the hands that had caused me so much pain in my life. But now I was holding the hands of a brother in Christ. I struggled to hold back the tears.

He was a brother in Christ before he was my dad. I held those hands, and it was good. It was more than good, it was wonderful. It was a gift from the Lord. A brother in Christ…. My dad.

After reading this book, could you have ever imagined that my dad would know Jesus? I called him the next day and had another good but hard conversation about end-of-life details. He told me he thought his pacemaker was the only thing keeping him alive. I said I thought it's the Lord allowing him time to reconcile before he's gone. He agreed and it was good.

They drained eighteen pounds of liquid off of his legs and did what they could, but they needed the bed and sent him home. This was a strange couple of weeks for me and my wife. This was so unexpected it was hard to know how to process it all. My wife wanted to believe it was true, but struggled a little. The Lord finally led her to want to see him again, and she was supporting me in continuing to see how he was doing. I hate to admit I didn't see him in person again until about a month later, but I had spoken to him on the phone several times to check on him. We decided to go and see him one Sunday after church. It was good to visit him at his home, and see where he lived. Remember, we had had nearly no contact for many years, and a lot had changed. Again, it was a good conversation, but he wasn't feeling well that day.

The next morning, I got a call that he had to be rushed to the ER in the middle of the night. I went to see him at the hospital and the doctors said there really wasn't anything more they could do for him, except to try and keep him comfortable. They were putting him on hospice and sending him home. I told my dad that if his pastors planned on praying with him, I would love to be involved. A few days later, one of my dad's pastors called me and we set a date to pray with him. We met and prayed, and it was good.

We read 1 Peter 1:3-9: *"Blessed be the God and Father of our Lord Jesus Christ! According to His great mercy, He has caused us to be born again to a living hope through the resurrection of Jesus Christ from the dead to an inheritance that is imperishable, undefiled, and unfading, kept in heaven for you, who by God's power are being* guarded through faith for a salvation ready to be revealed in the last time. In this you rejoice, though now for a little while, if necessary, you have been grieved by various trials, so that the tested genuineness of your faith—more precious than gold that perishes though it is tested by fire—may be found to result in praise and glory and honor at the revelation of Jesus Christ. Though you have not seen Him, you love Him. Though you do not now see Him, you believe in Him and rejoice with joy that is inexpressible and filled with glory, obtaining the outcome of your faith, the salvation of your souls."

We then talked about Matthew 18: 23-35: "Therefore the kingdom of heaven may be compared to a king who wished to settle accounts with his servants. When he began to settle, one was brought to him who owed him ten thousand talents. And since he could not pay, his master ordered him to be sold, with his wife and children and all that he had, and payment to be made. So the servant fell on his knees, imploring him, 'Have patience with me, and I will pay you everything.' And out of pity for him, the master of that servant released him and forgave him the debt. But when that same servant went out, he found one of his fellow servants who owed him a hundred denarii, and seizing him, he began to choke him, saying, 'Pay what you owe.' So his fellow servant fell down and pleaded with him, Have patience with me, and I will pay you.' He refused and went and put him in prison until he should pay the debt. When his fellow servants saw what had taken place, they were greatly distressed, and they went and reported to their master all that had taken place. Then his master summoned him and said to him, 'You wicked servant! I forgave you all that debt because you pleaded with me. And should not you have had mercy on your fellow servant, as

I had mercy on you?' And in anger his master delivered him to the jailers, until he should pay all his debt. So also my heavenly Father will do to every one of you, if you do not forgive your brother from your heart."

Matthew 18 convicted me. God had forgiven me of much, and I needed to forgive my dad. I meditated on Matthew 18 all week and it was good for me to do so. My wife has forgiven my dad also. For me to see her have forgiveness and compassion for my dad is so powerful. At the end of my dad's life to reconcile with not only me, but others as well, is mind blowing. When he calls, I no longer have that dread… I have peace. I no longer have the hate…I have love. It's still a little strange, but you know what? That's OK. I don't have to worry about it, because God has this in His hands.

I heard an Alistair Begg sermon where he talks about the thief on the cross entering heaven, and the angels asking him how he got there. The thief says he doesn't know how he got there except, the man on the middle cross said he could come. I see that simple faith in my dad. He doesn't know all the things most Christians know. He hasn't done all the studies and things most Christians do. All he knows is, "The man on the middle cross said he could come too." And I say, "Amen! And thank you Lord."

My dad passed away Christmas Day 2024. The last words he said to me were "I love you son." I don't remember him ever saying those words to me before.

God is so good. Never underestimate Him and what He might be doing in your life, or the lives of those around you. Don't let pride get in your way of seeing His glory and majesty as He works in your life.

My story—I mean, God's story—isn't over yet. Thank you Jesus, for walking with me through my life. Thank you for helping me to be brave.

L.W.E.
July 2, 2025

www.ingramcontent.com/pod-product-compliance
Lightning Source LLC
Chambersburg PA
CBHW010938120626
46554CB00008B/2520